THE GLOBALIST AGENDA IS STILL REAL AND DANGEROUS

The great friendship between the Great Reset and the Covid-19 continues

Part 2

The globalist agenda is still real and dangerous. The great friendship between the Great Reset and the Covid-19 continues. Part 2.

Written by César Andrés Muñoz Madrigal between March and April 2021.

L'Hospitalet de Llobregat, Barcelona, Spain.

CONTENTS

Foreword

Having written the book "The Globalist Agenda is real, man-made and dangerous. The great friendship between the Great Reset and the Covid-19 " in January 2021, with regard to the globalist agenda, events and meetings have continued to take place, since they are fully active elites that promote this agenda little by little, so the tycoons of technological companies, financial elites, politicians, etc. who are behind this agenda continuously develop new concepts, events, put out books, publish articles, etc. in order to raise awareness and mentally prepare society little by little towards where it wants them to go, since as they well know many of their globalist projects and ideas are not going to be to the liking of people at first.

Thus the authors of the globalist agenda today speak of new concepts and projects such as inclusive capitalism, cyber pandemic, sustainability of technological ecosystems, the Green New Deal in the United States, inclusive, sustainable and resilient policies in an environment where the gender perspective is respected and protected, etc. and therefore it was necessary to talk about all these new projects and concepts with a second part to the first book on the globalist agenda.

I have also seen it necessary to update and add information on these globalist events, meetings and projects in which the same characters almost always appear around the globalist round table, sometimes under the umbrella of new names and acronyms of organizations but almost always being the same actors, backed by the Catholic pope on duty, which in this case is Pope Francis, the large investment funds, the main pharmaceutical, financial, technological companies, the Rockefeller foundation, the Rothschild family, the George Soros foundation and their NGOs , etc. and at the top of which are the members of the Group of the 30 or G30 who are mostly bankers.

Also I have also seen it necessary to add more information about the Microsoft and vaccine magnate, Bill Gates, whose performance and influence encompasses every aspect of the globalist agenda, including the global warming theory, the Global Vaccination Alliance (Gavi), the information verification Alliance or "fact-checking", the ID2020 digital identity project developed by the Digital Identity Alliance, etc.

In this way, not only is this globalist technocracy always present in most of the events of the globalist agenda, but they also support each other to develop and implement this supremacist agenda, despite the fact that there may have rivalries and opposed interests which simply makes this agenda take longer to implement or temporarily to fail one of their projects.

But despite its setbacks, this globalist agenda is accelerating with the help of the arrival of Covid-19, as indicated and desired by the president of the World Economic Forum, Klaus Schwap, in his book "Covid-19: the Great Reset". This Great Reset promoted by the Davos Forum (the World Economic Forum usually meets every year in the town of Davos, Switzerland) is today the visible execution of the globalist agenda, and it is only necessary to go to its website to confirm that the plans of these globalist oligarchies are not only real, but are being updated almost every week with new concepts and projects that in theory are for the good of humanity as they advocate.

Therefore, in the face of the acceleration in the implementation of the globalist agenda which is visible all through the World Economic Forum and in its Great Reset project, it has also been necessary to add new information to the first book that I wrote about the globalist agenda.

Introduction and presentation of the general scenario

As we saw in the first part of this book, the dogmas of the globalist agenda are:

1. The theory of global warming, now called climate change.
2. The LGTBIQ + ideology
3. Extreme feminism
4. The abortion.
5. Euthanasia.
6. Mass and uncontrolled immigration
7. The legalization of drugs

In this way, the previous dogmas help in the achievement of the objectives of the globalist agenda, basically managing to create tension within the nations, to justify the implantation of a supranational government, the elimination of the sovereignty of the nations and the emptying of their identity and own culture as nations.

We must also remember that the globalist oligarchies have their own agenda, the objectives of which are summarized as predictions in the 2030 Agenda on a video that can be found on the World Economic Forum website which are as follows:

1. "You will have nothing and you will be happy. You will be able to rent things you need and a drone will take them home for you. "

2. "The United States will not be the world's leading superpower.

3. "You will not die waiting for an organ donor: they will be manufactured with 3D printers."

4. "You will eat much less meat: meat will be "an occasional treat, not a staple, for the sake of the environment and our health. "

5. "One billion people will have to be displaced by climate change.

6. "Polluters will have to pay to emit carbon dioxide. There will be a global price for carbon dioxide. This will help fossil fuels to come to past. "

7. "Scientists are working towards a healthy stay in space, which can facilitate research."

8. "Western values will be put to the test. The values that sustain our democracies must be considered."

While in this second book we are going to see how the globalist agenda begins with the deception of the monetary and financial system that creates money out of thing air (out of nothing) by the central banks and allows nations to borrow more and more money in order to increase the public expenditure; and in turn this public debt ultimately has to be paid by taxpayers of the middle classes through taxes, which progressively impoverishes them. Just above the central banks in the pyramid of power we find the group of 30, G30, which is basically made up of central bank bankers and of the large international banks, whose executing agency is the bank of central banks, that is the Bank for International Settlements.

We will also discover that financial elites want to eliminate cash to control us even more through the creation of government-backed Fiat digital currencies, and that cryptocurrencies are therefore a good option to escape this control imposed by globalist oligarchies.

We will also analyze the figure of Bill Gates, the founder of Microsoft, a philanthropist who has actively participated in the definition of that unique thought of the globalist agenda that invades us today, through his projects at the Bill and Melinda Gates Foundation, the Alliance for Global Vaccination (Gavi), the lie and truth about the microchips of Bill Gates's vaccines that are not actually in vaccines but in contraceptive pills, synthetic DNA, his defense of measures to stop the supposed global warming and Microsoft's alliance with newspapers, technological companies and news networks, together with the financing of the "Big Tech", the biggest technological companies, known as GAFTA (Google, Apple, Facebook, Twitter and Amazon) etc. to verify the truth of the news, known as "fact-checking".

In addition, we will also discover how in all this spiderweb of alliances, new concepts and globalist projects there are always practically the same actors sitting around the table of the globalist agenda, who use constant fear to control the population: to the Covid-19 pandemic the cyberpandemics will follow, as Klaus Schwap, the president of the World Economic Forum, has already said, possibly followed in turn by a green swan crisis, which will be a climate crisis as indicated on the Bank for International Settlements.

Part 1. <u>On the monetary and financial system that drives the globalist agenda</u>

2

The origin of the globalist agenda: the deception of the monetary expansion and of the perpetual debt

Some economists and financial specialists call financial alchemy or modern alchemy the process of converting paper into money, by the work and grace of bankers with the privileges granted by politicians and the issuance of money without backing in materials such as gold or savings. Alchemy was a pseudoscience that defended the conversion of lead into gold, which It is possible to do but very expensive though, being it is cheaper to buy the gold directly from the market.

In fact, very few people know what is behind the world monetary system and, therefore, they are not aware of whom is responsible for the recurring economic crises, which makes it impossible to carry out the necessary reforms to avoid recessions and end this great larceny. Because it is really a great global scam, the most important, because all the others of the globalist agenda emanate from it.

This financial alchemy refers to the fact that central banks create money out of thin air without the backing of materials or people's savings.

This current financial system that creates money without backing is made for people who do not know it and that central banks and governments take advantage of the middle and poor classes.

In this way the money has come out based on trial and error with the participation of people without the mediation of any state. At first it arose to cover exchange needs with barter, which was a means of direct exchange, that is, one merchandise was exchanged for another, but later the States have wanted to take advantage of it by minting their own currency. This money issued by the states is based on the trust that people place in it.

At first, with barter, for example, a baker had to go to the butcher and pay the butcher with a loaf of bread. Obviously, this system presents many problems, among them what happens if the butcher does not want bread.

This is how they began to pay with gold and silver, since they perfectly fulfilled the functions of money: they are a reserve of value, they are divisible, they are easily transportable and It was possible to make exchanges with them.

Later, in the late Middle Ages and in the Modern Age, the Venetian nobility accepted the deposit of gold, which was the money of the time, and in return issued documents that the person who had deposited the gold had the right to receive an amount of money in gold in the future. But this nobility and the lenders and borrowers realized that it was easier to transport these documents than the gold itself to pay, so these right-of-payment documents became the future paper money.

Above all because the United States was the nation that had made the Allies win in World War II and because since it had not been bombed, it could afford to help economically to rebuild Europe after World War II. In addition, the Bretton Woods agreements agreed to link the dollar to gold, for $35 an ounce of gold, but with the increasing expenses of the American State during the 50s and 60s, its economy ended up heavily indebted at the end of the 60s and at the beginning of the 70s and the price of the dollar therefore had fallen a lot, so nations like France bought gold instead of dollars, and a black market had even been created in which an ounce of gold was sold for $45 an ounce, that is, 10 dollars above the official price.

To this day and especially since the time of the former president of the United States, Barak Obama, it has been published in alternative media that United States was going to return to the gold standard, but it has not been like that, although it seemed that Trump intended to partially link the dollar to gold.

In addition to this there are still publications in the present that seem to have a New Age influence which basically say that good spirits will bring us a new Nesara-Gesara monetary system. NESARA stands for National Economic Security and Recovery Act and was a set of proposed economic reforms for the United States suggested during the 1990s by Harvey Francis Barnard. Barnard claimed that the proposals, which included replacing the income tax with a national sales tax, abolishing compound interest on secured loans, and returning to a bimetallic currency, would result in 0% inflation and a more stable economy. The proposals were never introduced before Congress and has since become better known as the subject of a cult-like conspiracy theory as Wikipedia says.

So the Nesara-Gesara monetary system was meant to be the return to the gold standard along with the implementation of a new quantum financial system, which has not occurred and is simply a hoax on the part of groups that can be considered controlled dissent, and that could perfectly be part of a United States military counterintelligence service, so that basically people think that everything is under control and that it is not necessary to demonstrate or fight for anything.

This type of messages referring to some aliens or good spirits that in "the Great Awakening" of humanity (which by the way is also the name of an occult organization of the nineteenth century) would bring us the Nesara-Gesara monetary system, the quantum financial system, etc. abound in the information channels related to the QAnon (Q) movement, which in theory are in favor of Donald Trump, but which after the presidential elections of November 3, 2020, have been a channel of disinformation saying that Trump had everything controlled at all times to be the president of the United States despite the fact that there had been a massive electoral fraud that caused him to lose the elections.

In fact, as I recently wrote in the book "The Great American Conspiracy. The elections that changed democracy", there was a conspiracy for Trump to lose the elections by unions, Big Tech (big technology corporations), businessmen, etc. as "the Time" magazine itself has published, but Trump was never able to reverse this situation despite what these alternative media said, nor was he ever in control of it.

In this way money has always been necessary and even in the times when it was eliminated, substitutes such as tobacco have been sought, for example, as in prisons or in occupied Germany in the Second World War, since General Dwight Eisenhower prohibited payment in German currency because it contained an inscription with the Nazi swastika.

So the problem is that central banks issue money out of thin air especially to buy the public debt of the States, finance the holes in the banks that lend more money than they have in the treasury thanks to the so-called fractional reserve, that is to say, they can lend more money than they have. In this way the fractional reserve in Europe can be of a maximum of 1%, that is to say that with 1 euro for example they could lend up to 99, while in the United States the fractional reserve is up to a maximum of 10%.

In this way, central banks create money from nothing or buy sovereign debt from States, and private banks also create money from nothing when they lend more money than they have, which causes a financial bubble in which there are more and more money in the market which causes inflation, but most people ignore that this public debt of the nations and deficits of the states are ultimately passed on in the form of taxes to the middle and lower classes.

In this way, inflation is very difficult to stop and can only be counteracted by raising interest rates so that there is less money flow in the market, but if interest rates are raised when there is inflation and an economic crisis, as it happens in the present time generated by the Covid-19 pandemic, then the price of the dollar would sink and the economy would collapse.

Thus, to solve these financial bubbles of monetary expansion, understanding as monetary expansion the creation of more and more money without support in people's savings, they are compensated in turn by creating more financial bubbles and with more economic expansion, and thus the economy is connected to an assisted breathing machine.

As the founding fathers of the United States have already warned, a nation should not go into debt because who owes money is the slave of its creditor, which is what the Bible itself tells.

In this way in the book of Proverbs of the bible it says: "The rich rule over the poor and the debtor is the slave of the creditor" Proverbs 22: 7, which is truth both for private individuals or for States.

In this regard there is also a quote from Henry Ford that illustrates this very well which says: " It is well enough that people of the nation do not understand our banking and monetary system, for if they did, I believe there would be a revolution before tomorrow morning".

In this way, the system of creating money from nothing without any support is an oppressive and impoverishing means of the middle and lower classes who end up paying more and more taxes in order to support a growing State that gets indebted more and more and in order to support banks. that make people more and more indebted to them through their loans.

Thus, Klaus Schwab, the president of the World Economic Forum, which is the entity that is currently standing up for the globalist agenda, in his book published in June 2020 entitled "Covid-19: the Great Reset", already talks about this saying: "The state will try to exert its influence over the central banks to finance important public projects and in the same way it is possible that the precept that the State may intervene to maintain employment, the income of workers and avoid the bankruptcy of companies last when these policies come to an end ". In other words, Klaus Schwab is saying that public and political pressure is likely to continue for this type of measure to persist, thus supporting continued monetary expansion,

In this way the globalist entities such as the World Economic Forum, the World Bank, the central banks, the Bank for International Settlements, etc. do not want to free us from this deceptive and enslaving financial and monetary system but they intend to increase it and perpetuate it over time.

In a similar way, these supranational globalist entities intend to finish with the dollar as a monetary reserve and with the monetary system as it is assembled today, causing through monetary expansion an inflation in which prices will rise exponentially, which in turn will create even more impoverishment of most of the population.

In addition, these globalist oligarchies intend to finish with the cash through the creation of so-called digital currencies that we should not confuse with cryptocurrencies such as Bitcoin.

It may be thought that with the elimination of cash, money laundering and trafficking in women or pedophilia will disappear, but it is proved that corruption cases continue to be committed today with payment through debit and credit cards anyways, and that payment through digital means does not prevent money laundering.

Ultimately, the current financial system of continuous monetary expansion shifts costs through taxes to the middle and poor classes, which is robbery upon robbery, and simply helps to create a global socialist system where nations are increasingly poor and governed by supranational entities such as the World Economic Forum that would direct global politics and economy.

In this way, with the excuse that social aid must be given to alleviate the crises that these financiers and supranational oligarchies cause, the States are increasingly indebted to enslave and impoverish the middle and lower classes.

3

Bitcoin versus digital currencies

As many of us know well, the value of Bitcoin has risen in recent months especially when the current richest man in the world, Elon Musk, declared in February 2021 that he had invested $ 1 billion in bitcoin. Thus, on April 13, 2021, the bitcoin traded at a record price of $ 63,588.20 per bitcoin.

So bitcoin is the star cryptocurrency, but there are many other cryptocurrencies besides bitcoin. It is a digital currency that is not issued by central banks, which is independent of the States and anonymous, since when paying or selling with bitcoins, the names of the people who make the purchase and sale transactions do not appear.

Bitcoin transactions are carried out through software and an algorithm. To carry out these buying and selling operations or other transactions, a public key and a private key are needed. The public key would be the address of the wallet or purse in which the money is going to be received and the private key is the one that people need in order to open that box or wallet of the person to whom we want to send bitcoins or pay to. When bitcoins are sent to the recipient, they can verify if they have received those bitcoins by opening their wallet with their private key.

Bitcoins do not travel from one computer to another or from one wallet to another, because being a digital system based on blockchain or on blockchain technology, the transaction is recorded in a global digital database.

Thousands of copies of these transactions are registered on the servers of the users who act as miners. In this way there is a global database of which copies of it are made in a multitude of cryptocurrency miner devices. In this way this system is protected because it is decentralized and at the same time nobody can alter it because many miners have a copy of its original.

The fundamental difference is that we have a record in our bank of our deposit, of our transactions, of our movements, but with bitcoin there is a common record for everyone, decentralized and that cannot be controlled by anyone and that may be verified by any miner anytime.

Thus, it can be verified that an operation with bitcoin has occurred but what cannot be known is the identity of both people who made the transaction. In this way the identity is never known since the system it is operating all the time with a digital numerical account.

By the way miners are people who at first were at home with a computer and have now become professional by putting their computer equipment to work to validate these cryptocurrency transactions, that is, by sending bitcoins to another person or company, what the blockchain system does is sending that operation to the miners who compete through their software to be the ones who sign that transaction, that is the miners compete to be the notary of that transaction and once the transaction is executed it is registered in the blockchain system.

In this way we have tens of thousands of connected computers mining at the same time. In fact there is a study from the University of Cambridge that says that bitcoin alone consumes 88 tera watts per hour of electricity per year, which is more or less the electricity consumption per year of Belgium.

So the price of electricity in a nation does influence the number of miners that may be in that country, and so most of the miners are in China because electricity is much cheaper there and therefore they have an extra incentive to mine bitcoins.

In addition, the higher the price of the bitcoins, the greater incentive so that there may be more miners, since they are all paid with bitcoins.

Using blockchain technology is a more secure payment system than the traditional financial system, and the miners compete to have greater processing capacity and better servers because the more processing power, the greater the possibility of being able to be the one validating an operation with bitcoins.

The problem with cryptocurrencies and blockchain technology is that it is difficult to understand for those who are not computer scientists, that is, its way of operating is not intuitive and also is quite well known that there are often news of the theft of bitcoins in exchanges, which are businesses that allow customers to trade cryptocurrencies or digital currencies for other assets, such as conventional fiat money or other digital currencies. In fact these exchanges are from time to time hacked and their bitcoins stolen, as the exchanges are in charge of managing users' bitcoins and safeguarding their private keys. In this manner it would often be better if we printed several copies of our private keys, which are convertible to QR code in order to avoid depositing our keys in a bitcoin exchange which could be stolen.

A third problem with cryptocurrencies and especially bitcoin is that they are not good value reserve assets since they are subject to a lot of volatility in their price.

However, on the other hand, central banks are promoting what are called fiat digital currencies, which are often confused with cryptocurrencies, but which are basically issued by central banks, and which may or may not be linked to gold or other materials. The directors of these central banks justify the creation of these fiat digital currencies with the fact of adapting transaction operations to the new technologies, but in fact it does not make sense because today's operations are already carried out digitally through the use of debit or credit cards for example.

In this way, the true unconfessed reason for the creation of digital currencies is to put an end to cash and thus be able to control people on what and how they spend their money, so that the state and globalist supranational governments may be able to tell them what they should and should not buy or consume.

In fact, cash together with cryptocurrencies is one of the few ways that we still have so that they do not control what and how we spend money on and are ways to preserve our minimum individual freedom, since if the cash disappears we will not be able to withdraw money from the bank in case banks start to charge us negative interests or high commissions for example, which unfortunately is already happening in some banks in the Nordic countries of Europe where customers are being charged negative interest for having their money in bank accounts, that is the customers are paying to the banks for keeping their money.

In fact, negative interest rates are the consequence of the continuous monetary expansion that creates money without the backing of gold, other materials or people's savings, and shows that the money of the future will be worth less than today's, so saving is discouraged, which in turn is exactly what central banks and globalist organizations also promote, that is, they promote consumption and not saving, which collides head-on with the situation in which today we are: restrictions on people's movements and on business opening times, etc. which in turn causes an economic crisis that limits the very consumption due to people's uncertainty about the future, lack of work, establishments with limited hours and restrictions, businesses that have gone bankrupt or shut down, the partial closure of borders for travelling, etc. In summary, none of these factors help in order to reactivate consumption again.

In this way, if the cash disappears and the cryptocurrencies also disappear then when the banks begin to charge us negative interests for having open accounts with them and having our money deposited there, there will be no way of being able to get rid of them taking away our little savings. In fact, the forecast is that it will be legislated in the short-medium term so that the banks will be able to charge commissions to their customers, and thus instead of charging negative interests to their bank deposits, customers will pay commissions justified as management and maintenance account fees.

17

4

The Group of Thirty or G30

The Group of 30 as they like to call themselves on their own website is a fairly unknown group. The name of the Group of 30, recalls the 30 silver coins that Zacharias prophesied on the bible and that Judas received as payment for betraying Jesus, but it also recalls the 30 tyrants of the government of Athens.

In this way the G30 is one of the instruments created and financed by the Rockefeller Foundation and it is a group of bankers, academics and politicians who run the world's finances in the shadows in a discreet manner. The directors of the management companies of the three large investment funds, the "Big Three", are part of the G30 which are: Black Rock, Vanguard and State Street Corporation, which are also the main shareholders of the main vaccine-creating companies such as Pfizer or Moderna. Along with the Big Three, we could also add Fidelity as one of the world biggest investment funds.

Also part of the G30 are the executives of large investment banks or "Big Bank" such as JP Morgan, Goldman Sachs and Deutsche Bank, etc.

In addition, the G30 is a private non-profit institution in theory, which is difficult to believe considering that it is made up of bankers and has a determining importance in the progress of the planetary economy and is one of the instruments created and financed by the Rockefeller Foundation, being one level above in the hierarchy of world power over the large investment fund managers, the central banks or the large investment banks mentioned above.

Its official name is the Consultative Group on International Economic and Monetary Affairs and it is based in Washington, United States.

Its members hold regular meetings, produce highly influential reports, setting the path to be followed by governments and financial companies with whom they share the table and tablecloth (another way of saying that they hold meetings together in order to plan how to control the world's finances).

In the Group of 30 there are directors of the Bank for International Settlements, which is an institution based in Basel and which acts as the Central Bank of central banks.

Although many may think that it is a Western group, the truth is that China and other Asian countries also have representatives, along with the ones from Russia. So it seems that in some way these countries may be taking advantage to attend as listeners, although many times they have a voice and no vote, although in reality the monetary policy of Russia or China does not have much to do with that of Europe, with that of United States, with that of the UK or with that of other Western countries that have members present in the Group of 30.

Its members meet and make decisions without lights or stenographers, and the truth is that it is almost impossible to find content of their meetings on the internet. Moreover like it happens with the World Economic Forum, the members of the G30 when making decisions usually meet in hotels.

There are people who access recordings of these meetings on the internet, although it is not known whether they do it on the dark web or on very specialized pages, but there are people who seem to assure that they have accessed some of these partial recordings of the G30 meetings.

As It has already been said, the members of the G30 manage the global fiduciary monetary system from the shadows and, of course, having privileged information. Who are its members?. So if we go to the website of the Group of 30 and we look at it, they are just central bank governors, directors of the International Monetary Fund, of the World Bank, the Bank for International Settlements, secretaries of the Treasury, finance ministers, as well as economists with great prestige among the left such as the American Paul Krugman.

There are also members of the large investment banks who may be still working in their positions or that may no longer be active, although many of them are currently in the main centers of the world monetary power.

That is, the G30 is not a body where those who have retired tend to go but there are also people who are currently occupying active professional positions such as the current United States Secretary of the Treasury, Janet Yellen, the current Italian Prime Minister, Mario Draghi, who previously was President of the European Central Bank.

In this way they act as a kind of political office for financial planning, intervening in interest rates and helping investment banks and some commercial banks to act, like the instruments of an orchestra in which the G30 takes the lead and participates in the sheet music design. In this way we have just said that the G30 participates in the design of the scores (sheet music design) because the scores are surely designed in a higher step of the pyramid.

The current leadership of the G30 is led by Jacob Frenkel, who is the president of the investment bank JP Morgan Chase, is also a member of the globalist body the Trilateral Commission and was a former governor of the Bank of Israel. In addition, he has been awarded the title of Knight of the Great Italian Cross.

In addition, some consider that Jacob Frenkel also serves the interests of the black nobility, which would be the base of the global crime syndicate that controls this planet. The black nobility or the black aristocracy are the aristocratic families who sided with the Pope Pius IX after the army of the Kingdom of Italy led by the Savoy family entered Rome on September 20, 1870, it overthrew the Pope and the Papal States, and took over the Quirinal Palace and the nobles later ennobled by the previous Pope signed the Lateran Treaty in 1929. So it is said that any family that produces Popes for the Vatican is part of the royalty and in this way most of the black nobility are Vatican royalty. The black nobility considers themselves sovereign princes.

These families earned the title of "black" nobility for their relentless unscrupulousness. They used murder, rape, kidnapping, robbery and all kinds of deception on a large scale, without resisting the achievement of their objectives.

Thus, according to writers such as Daniel Estulin, the Vatican is used a little bit as an intelligence network, which within the Group of 30 it also seems to be the case with the Society of Jesus itself (the Jesuits), the Scythians, the Order of Malta and the Knights of Columbus among others.

If we also look more deeply at the biography of Jacob Frenkel we happen to discover that he was vice president of the American International Group, AIG, which was the large insurance company rescued by the Barack Obama government after the bankruptcy of Lehman Brothers which on the contrary was not rescued.

In this way, if we analyze the trajectory of Jacob Frenkel, he has been in practically all the centers of financial power in the world, being also the president of the investment bank Merrill Lynch International, a bank that was bought by Bank of America, and that was rescued precisely also in 2008 thanks to US taxpayer money.

The Group of 30 also has a Spaniard among its Board of Directors, Jaime Caruana, who was governor of the Bank of Spain and president of the Bank for International Settlements, like many other members of the G30 have also been directors of the Bank for International Settlements.

Mario Draghi is also part of the G30, who has been also responsible for this group becoming relatively famous because when he was president of the European Central Bank, the European Ombudsman presented a document with a request for him to leave the G30 because considered that there was an obvious conflict of interest, but in fact in most supranational globalist entities there are still people in charge of governments, institutions or banks who would have conflicts of interest.

But in the end the European Parliament ruled that Mario Draghi could belong to the G30, be president of the European Central Bank and be perfectly the Italian president at the same time, regardless of any conflict of interest.

Another prominent member of the G30 is Mark Carney, who was governor of the Central Bank of Canada, later governor of the Bank of England and who began his career at the investment bank Goldman Sachs, where he spent 13 years, surely being prepared to assume his current mission. In this way the investment banks Goldman

Sachs and JP Morgan have always had payroll workers who would later become bastions of the globalist agenda.

Thus, in June 2019, before the arrival of the Covid-19 pandemic, as governor of the Bank of England, Mark Carney gave a speech in London predicting the future after the Covid-19 pandemic, and so we can verify to what extent the reality that we are living in these days has been planned, developed and simmered for a long time. In this way Carney said: "A new economy is emerging driven by changes in technology, demographics and the environment, and this economy requires new financing, new financing in the service of the digital economy. New financing with products that are more profitable, better adapted and more inclusive.

New funding to support the transition to a sustainable economy. New financing that balances innovation with resilience. With its leadership in fintech and green finance, the UK private sector is creating the new finance. The time is now. "

Fortunately it seems that this fusion of finance and false ecology is failing, so it is not giving the expected results and this global elite seems to be nervous about it. In fact, there is a disinformation campaign to make public opinion believe that the green transition should be accelerated.

So this acceleration seems to be a proven fact with the book that Bill Gates published in February 2021 entitled "How to avoid a climate disaster" along with the book by the Canadian author Naomi Klein, "On Fire". In this sense, I think that they want to anticipate this green transition because they thought that there would be a lot of time to take advantage of the situation of the Covid-19 pandemic, but they are seeing that their time is getting shorter and that at some point the idea that they may be able to use the pandemic to justify and promote any type of measure may fail, whether it may be the transition to green energy, or the restriction of individual rights or the restrictions upon businesses, etc.

In addition, the Rothschild family also had a fundamental role in the creation of the G30, and one of the members of this family, Lady Lynn de Rothschild not only belongs to the G30 but also belongs to the group of our guardians of The Council for the Inclusive Capitalism to which the Catholic Pope Francis also belongs.

They also appointed Geoffrey Bell, a man from the London School of Economics, as the first president of the G30, an institution founded by the Fabian society and that has recently promoted economists from the Soros school, such as the member of the

European Parliament Luis Garicano, who also usually appears in these kind of globalist programs.

In fact, the Fabian society had a wolf in sheep's clothing as a shield, which is rather appropriate and it was not accidental, since they chose this image intentionally for the shield.

In addition to the occult involvement that obviously has its shield, also one of the reasons why this society has gone down in history is because it has participated in the intellectual creation of the welfare state, which is effectively a wolf in skin of lamb. In other words, the Welfare State is a wolf in sheep's clothing because with the promise of the state's assistance it is possible to have people enslaved and subjected through the payment of taxes to cover that assistance, as It is happening now almost all over the world.

Some authors even go further since they consider that this society has acted as a connecting platform for the Masonic World Project, that is to say that they have had a certain participation or that at least members of both societies have also been in meetings together.

The Fabian society has also had its part in the drawing of the first outlines of the globalist agenda that already took place at the end of the 19th century and at the beginning of the 20th century. These connections are obvious and as it happens today these connections may be spotted because the very same people who were important at that time went to most of the meetings of all the globalist groups, as was the case of the famous neurologist, creator of psychoanalysis, Sigmund Freud.

So these people were seen in the same places and this is not due to chance, as today it is no coincidence that Lady Lynn de Rothschild is next to Father Francisco in the group photo of the Council for Inclusive Capitalism

And also these elites are participating in the intellectual domain of the great universities, such as Oxford University, Cambridge, Yale, Harvard and in the global media. Well, in fact one of their economic pontiffs was John Maynard Keynes.

In this manner few know that Keynes wrote a review on a book written in 1936 by the two founders of the Fabian society, who are the Webb couple, whose book is called "Soviet Communism: a new civilization.", which does not happen to be a very thoughtful title, writing in his review that Stalin's result of communism was impressive.

Keynes himself, in his book "The general theory of employment, interest and money", in his introduction specifies that a model where this theory would be carried out perfectly would be in a totalitarian state. But although Keynes was not a liberal economist, today he would be more liberal than many finance ministers of some Western countries.

Thus, for a long time one of the characteristic elements of the globalist agenda has been to finish with the national sovereignty and the ability of citizens to be able to elect rulers who oppose the plans of social engineers, being the most important element of this sovereignty determining the monetary policy. Thus Mayer Rothschild said: "Give me control of a country's money supply and I will not care who makes its laws."

And so also Dr. Frank Peak said that the destiny of the coin is and always will be the destiny of a nation.

In this way it is necessary to get out of the dichotomy of political left and right and speak of globalism versus patriotism. So in fact the destiny of the currency is the destiny of a nation and if what we have is a group above the central banks determining the destiny of the nations, then we have the globalist agenda in action because we are talking about these supranational oligarchies wanting to coordinate everything, including the coordination of the central bank plans.

Likewise, the Bloomberg news agency has said that the Bank for International Settlements is one of the financial media outlets of reference because it is the executing agency of the G30 and the last bastion of the global technocracy.

This bastion of global technocracy, which is lead by the Group of 30, now with the arrival of the Covid has stepped on the accelerator so that thanks to the technological dependence of societies and the economic crisis caused by the great debt bubble, it takes advantage on launching new digital currencies, that is, the euro, the dollar, the digital yuan, etc. These digital currencies are the competition of bitcoin and they are the new element of financial repression by having as their unconfessed objective, the disappearance of cash. It is difficult though that the project to make cash disappear may be successful because there are many people who do not want the cash to disappear, whilst this project is failing in part in most nations where it has been launched except for China.

In China, a time has come when the new generation of today has practically gone from their parents living in the villages and with little presence of technological means in their homes to doing practically everything with their mobile devices using super Apps like WeChat,, which happen to be very convenient to pay with.

But the case of China is different from the fact of making cash disappear intentionally, because this would already imply the control of citizens at an absolute higher level.

Moreover the G30 has joined the gentlemen of the World Economic Forum who are the promoters of the Great Reset and in this manner in June 2020 the Global Consortium for Digital Governance was created, that is to say, that everyone should have a digital identity and everyone should use digital money, so it won't take more than the push of a button to control whole societies.

The G30 and especially this Global Consortium has placed a lot of emphasis on the issue of global control of the cryptocurrencies because they are the competition to digital currencies.

In fact, in this Global Consortium for Digital Governance, the same members that belong to the G30, to the World Economic Forum or to other globalist entities such as the president of the Spanish bank Banco Santander, which is Ana Botín, Jacob Frenkel, who is the president of the G30, and Mario Draghi, the current Prime Minister of Italy, belong to as well.

Thus, in January 2021, the G30 published a report presented by Mario Draghi in which it called on governments to facilitate a process of creative destruction in the Covid crisis, which won't allow the market to make adjustments between supply and demand, but instead attributing to the elites the configuration of this New Economy previously destroyed by political and economic decisions taken by themselves, that is by the G30.

And when we read their report between the lines, we realize that the G30 is asking governments to help them choose which businesses should survive and which should shut down to facilitate the transition to the new normal.

It is also clear from this report that the G30 wants to have a corporatist global social State and they say that the current moment offers the opportunity to accelerate the processes, which is the type of language that we have in all the statements of the globalist organizations.

In this way, this globalist oligarchy not only recommends but also gives instructions that they hope will be followed and to ensure compliance with the instructions they have important positions among their members.

Seemingly the next financial crisis is going to be sold not as a crisis produced by the Covid virus, but as a crisis caused by climate change which they have already named as the crisis of the green swan which could be the next project of the G30.

Thus, there is already a document from the Bank for International Settlements that uses this concept of the black swan, which its president Nassim Taleb uses to justify a global offensive in the financial sector. Taleb considers that the economic crisis derived from the Covid-19 is not a black swan crisis since it could be foreseen.

In this way there is a report about the Covid-19 that can be found on the website of the Bank for International Settlements , where the green swan appears already dressed in green explaining that the next crisis will be a weather crisis. In this way it seems that they are stepping on the accelerator to take advantage of the global warming theory.

In this way, at the 2020 World Economic Forum, Donald Trump said that globalists always demand the same thing, that is, absolute power to dominate, to transform and to control every aspect of our lives.

Thus, the G30 is a core group for these power-hungry planners who are asking us for help to apply a Great Reset and not precisely with good intentions, although they want to present themselves as good people who look out for the good interest and rights of people.

Part 2. <u>New projects, new concepts and the elite of the globalist agenda</u>

5

Council for Inclusive Capitalism

Thus, the best way for the globalist agenda not to be successful is for people to know that it is a giant with feet of clay and this agenda is manifested today in the context of the Great Reset, whose implementation has been accelerated due to the Covid, and whose social engineers have launched a series of events and measures with different slogans to the public opinion, of which the one of the "new normal" is perhaps the most famous, although there is also that of "build back better", that is, to rebuild better , which would be the slogan that corresponds to the Council for Inclusive Capitalism that we are going to examine.

The translation of inclusive capitalism derives from the original in English of the book of the president of the World Economic Forum, Klaus Schwap, Stakeholder Capitalism, which literally means capitalism of the interested parties, which translated in this way is quite poorly understood.

In this way as we mentioned in the previous chapter on the G30, Klaus Schwap, founder and president of the World Economic Forum, published a book that came out at the end of January 2021 with the title of: "Stakeholder capitalism: a global economy that works for progress, for people and for the planet."

According to the very same website of the World Economic Forum in an article on what inclusive capitalism is, it is explained according to textual words taken from Klaus Schwap's book on the matter: "That is the core of stakeholder capitalism: it is a form of capitalism in which the companies not only optimize short-term profits for shareholders, but also seek long-term value creation, taking into account the needs of all their stakeholders and society in general. "

If as soon as the pandemic began, we had Klaus Schwap's book entitled "Covid-19: The Great Reset", now we have another glimpse of capitalism, as we can see how they are guiding us through this new world that they intend to configure. Although we have had the aperitif in December 2020, with the creation of the Council for Inclusive

Capitalism, which is an initiative led by the Vatican, whose godfather is the Pope Francisco and whose godmother is Lady Lynn Forester de Rothschild.

In this way the members of the globalist agenda no longer hide as they used to, as David Rockefeller himself said in an intervention at the Bilderberg Club, who thanked the mainstream media for not having told anything about their meetings, and for not shedding any light about them because in that way they were able to advance, which otherwise would have been impossible if the media would have fulfilled their reporting obligation.

In addition in the website of the Council for Inclusive Capitalism there is a photo in which Lady Lynn is beside Pope Francisco, whilst the members of the Council for Inclusive Capitalism are called the guardians of inclusive capitalism or "our guardians".

In the words of Pope Francisco Bergoglio himself, the group's goal is to make capitalism a more inclusive tool for the integral human well-being. Although this integral human well-being is decided by the Pope himself with Lady Lynn de Rothschild and not by God of course. Therefore, it is an integral human well-being that may not correspond to what others consider as integral human well-being. In other words, what a person may consider integral human well-being may not be the same as for another person.

In this way we confirm again that God has nothing to do with the Vatican and has never had anything to do with it.

Lady Lynn de Rothschild said in the presentation of this group that capitalism has caused the degradation of the planet and that the Council for Inclusive Capitalism will follow the recommendations of Father Francisco in this regard.

Moreover Lady Lynn says literally that we must listen to the cry of the Earth and the cry of the poor to design more equitable and sustainable growth models.

This crying of the Earth sounds to a marketing campaign to protect the Amazonas Jungle against the man-made deforestation and to old paganism where the Earth is worshiped instead of God, and the planet Earth is considered as a living god who suffers the mistreatment of human beings.

Related to this paganism in one of the currencies issued by the Vatican, which the Vatican has been doing for a long time in order to make some money, it turns out that the Pachamama appears, that is a lady with indigenous features who is pregnant of the

Earth. So the design from an artistic point of view is impeccable but the message is full of paganism.

Also in the Council for Inclusive Capitalism there is representation of many big multinational companies, along with the president of the Rockefeller Foundation who is Rajiv Shah; the president of State Street Corporation, which is one of the world's biggest investment funds; Mark Carney, who was the Head of the Bank of England and is now the United Nations Special Representative for Climate Action and Finance, bringing these two disciplines together.

But in addition to these people there are members of the Big Tech, the Big Bank, members of the world unions, that is to say that we have the list of usual suspects in the entities and meetings of the globalist agenda.

Moreover the presidents of Visa and Mastercard are part of the Council for Inclusive Capitalism, which seems a contradiction since Visa and Mastercard are two multinationals that rather represent the values of capitalism as always.

In addition, Mastercard also collaborates with Bill Gates in the ID2020 (Digital Identity 2020) project that aspires to digitally mark all humans on the planet.

Lady Lynn de Rothschild for her part is one of the people who belonged to the innermost circle of the pedophile Jeffrey Epstein. In this way Jeffrey Epstein said that Lady Lynn was a friend of his and that she introduced him to the one who eventually became Stein's lawyer. In this way, the one who was Stein's own lawyer, Alan Dershowitz said publicly that Mrs. Lynn of Rothschild was seeking contacts for Epstein, that is, that she opened doors for him. In fact, she introduced him to this quite prestigious jurist in the United States, who is the one who was on the team to defend former football player OJ Simpson.

Thus, the judgments and legal points of views that Alan Dershowitz holds are usually right and he is a very good connoisseur of the law but he is not a person precisely characterized by his ethics and he is also very well connected with the Zionist lobbies in the United States. In fact Dershowitz himself has Jewish ancestry and his last name is Jewish.

Lady Lynn is also good friends with the Bill and Hillary Clinton marriage and when she married another Rothschild, they spent at least one night on their honeymoon invited to the White House occupied at that time by the Clintons.

Although Pope Francis promised many things when he ascended the Pontifical throne, among others to put order in the Vatican accounts, he has not really put any order in these accounts and the Vatican bank is still used for money laundering operations.

For his part, the president of the Rockefeller Foundation Ravij Shah, who is part of the Council for Inclusive Capitalism, helped Bill and Melinda Gates in that project of the alliance for a green revolution in Africa, Agra, and which basically concluded with an increase of 30% of the number of people who went hungry by collapsing the already poor agricultural productivity of the African continent by introducing the famous genetically modified seeds, which only bear fruit on trees or sterile vegetation, that is that these trees are not able to reproduce themselves again.

Moreover Ravij Shah, the president of the Rockefeller Foundation, was also in the United States Agency for International Development. The USAID has also intervened in Africa and has also worked for Gavi, Bill Gates' alliance for global vaccination. Ravij Shah is now in charge of the Rockefeller Foundation and months after the arrival of the pandemic in June 2020 he published a report in which he proposed to transform the food supply in the United States, which he calls "reset the table", which is another globalist resetting project, precisely just after Bill Gates had talked about eating vegetable meat and Gates had just bought hectares of land in the United States, becoming the first large landowner in this nation. This "reset the table" is a project in order to transition to eating less meat and replacing it by eating plant-based meat and meat created in the laboratory.

In fact in the United States a lot of meat is consumed because among other things, it is relatively inexpensive and because it is also very easy to cook, that is after all a griddle on a grill is the simplest thing in the world.

So if with all these lands and farms that Bill Gates is buying they are going to dedicate themselves to exporting to other countries, surely It is going to be a good business but if it is intended to make North Americans change from a diet that is fundamentally carnivorous to a vegetarian diet, possibly Mr. Gates has little chance of success.

In this way in the meetings of the Council for Inclusive Capitalism as in other meetings of globalist entities, the need or demand to reform the global economic system is repeatedly raised, going with their ideas and projects far beyond personal freedom and elementary individual rights, a fact that almost nobody questions just because there is a pandemic, which is the great excuse for any reset.

In other words, they have succeeded in making individual rights or their defense taking a backseat and that people begin to embrace the possibility that there are rights that are not individual, that is global rights that are determined by people who are above the rest and that have the ability to determine what is right and what is wrong.

As always, these elites say that they do everything for our good, because cynicism is one of the fundamental characteristics of these social engineers. So even the French President Emmanuel Macron came out in his speech saying that capitalism cannot continue to be the system on which the relations of economic agents are based.

In this way, the most prominent politicians of nations such as the president of France himself are repeating the messages of globalist entities, introducing a concept that we are going to hear a lot in the coming months, which is the supposed disconnection between value creation and business and personal profits.

Unfortunately the worst of all is that these globalist messages are being launched whilst most of the people are unaware that the current system that has brought us to disaster has nothing to do with capitalism or freedom. In this way the globalist oligarchies have an open path to spread these type of message without great resistance and with a path that has already been paved or prepared for the people to accept it.

In this way at the 2020 World Economic Forum, the challenges of the economic system before the pandemic were put in common, being one of the most prominent and publicized interventions the one of Marc Benioff, billionaire founder of Salesforce, which is a cloud data company. Likewise, Marc Benioff announced the death of capitalism at the Davos Forum or World Economic Forum, being him precisely one of the people who has become a billionaire thanks to the current economic system.

Thus, the World Economic Forum has been transmitting this message for years that it is necessary to transition to another type of capitalism, and thus Marc Benioff at the 2018 Davos Forum said that "the concept of creating value for shareholders has been a driving force of the businesses that have been consolidated since companies went public but nevertheless, as companies and governments adapt to the new realities of the fourth industrial revolution, the idea that the greatest business success is the degree that enriches its shareholders is being questioned. "

In fact the same president of the World Economic Forum, Klaus Schwap, is a specialist and is obsessed with the Fourth Industrial Revolution as well as with the evolutionary leap of the human being made from the human being himself, what is known as transhumanism.

Now the Council for Inclusive Capitalism is spreading the message that the Covid-19 pandemic is a wonderful opportunity to launch a model in which large multinationals work hand in hand with governments. In this way the globalist finance magnate George Soros said in April 2020 that it was the crisis of his life.

In this way, now in theory would be the time to merge companies and States for the benefit of the general interest, whose antecedents of alliance between the State and large multinationals or corporations are in the Nazism of Adolf Hitler who copied it from the national corporatism of the Italian dictator Benito Mussolini.

Some authors go even further and even place the origins of this alliance or merger of states with large corporations at the dawn of the industrial revolution, when shipping and railroad companies allied themselves with governments.

In fact, there is an economist who studies corporate governance called Randall Morck, who puts this very well in recent studies, and explains that Hitler since he came to power, the first thing that he did was to exempt the managers of large companies from defending the interests of the shareholders with a law of 1937.

This was about the need for corporations, in whose head were the States, to be due to the general interest or to the so called common good, putting the interests of society ahead of those of the individuals.

But it is obvious where all this ends because if a manager does not respond to the shareholders, to the company owners and to the workers but to the political system, then companies cannot be efficient and the cases of corruption among company managers multiply, who agree with the State rulers to be granted public contracts in exchange for money bites from the profits made with these contracts.

In this way, when companies have benefits in a free market environment without important privileges, this indicates that this company or corporation is doing its job well, that is that it supplies goods and services with a good quality and at an adequate cost, which is the mission of a company, and when this goal is fulfilled then the companies make profits.

Thus we must differentiate the managers of multinational companies from the same multinationals for which they work. In other words, multinationals are not bad in themselves, but their managers are the ones who are often corrupt. So if we skipe the premise that when companies make money is just because they supply goods and services at an adequate quality and cost, then there is no economic calculation that is one of the keys to the failure of any statist planning system.

Although unfortunately there is an economic criterion, but not for the operation of the company but for how much the current account of the managers is going to increase. In addition to this the globalist oligarchies such as the Council for Inclusive Capitalism itself say that the current economic system is already over, it is already bankrupt, that it has fallen and that it has to be redefined.

That is why central banks are issuing money non-stop, that is why they are feeding bubbles one after another. So the elites know that now is the time to move to a system that does not prioritize free market or a system that prioritizes the control from large corporations and the State, because large corporations do not want competition either.

Now it seems to be the best time to finish with the small and medium competitors giving the fact that a circumstance such as the coronavirus epidemic has truly put it on a platter.

Of course if we want to dress a doll, we must first create prophets and place them on the same level as the fathers of previous economic systems. In this way the World Economic Forum has said that Klaus Schwap is the successor of the economist Milton Friedman and shows us in a table in the website of the World Economic Forum: State capitalism, shareholder capitalism and inclusive capitalism, in which allegedly the State capitalism was the capitalism of the beginning, then the father of shareholder capitalism was Milton Friedman and the father of inclusive capitalism is Klaus Schwap, who in 1971 created the Davos Forum, which in its own manifesto says that a new economic model is necessary.

Obviously putting the economist Milton Friedman and the founding social engineer of the World Economic Forum, Klaus Schwap, on the same level is not very accurate because the latter is not an economist at all to begin with.

Thus Klaus Schwap seems to draw the ideas from a book by the American editor of The Economist magazine, Mathew Bishop, so Klaus Schwap begins to argue that business groups have to be on the same level as states as promoters of social priorities, and the most remarkable thing is that he performs an argumentative pirouette, especially in relation to the need for a world government because in the first part of the book he admits that a planetary government would harm citizens and considers that it would not be feasible to defend its creation.

So it is about the idea of not telling the truth to the people, because if they are told the truth in everything they will not want to swap to this new model and there would be great opposition, which Klaus Schwap defines in his book as a lack of commitment on the part of the people.

In this way no matter how much they try to indoctrinate us, it is normal that the people do not believe the whole message straight away and refuse to change at the beginning.

Klaus Schwap also says in his book that local administrations are the ones that must make decisions about the day-to-day life of citizens, but that there are a series of matters over which supranational entities that impose global criteria must have competence. So they say that local entities should be able to decide for themselves, except when it is not feasible or effective for them to do so.

Who decides what local entities should decide and what supranational entities should decide?. It is decided by supranationalist entities of course and they spread their ideas through a series of transmission belts that go from the media outlets to social media platforms alongside institutions that are increasingly dedicated to it.

In Spain, for example, if we enter to the "Banco de Santander" website, all these messages that we are explaining here show up in their website and are the same as the ones of the Great Reset and the same as those on the World Economic Forum website, since Banco de Santander is absolutely committed to the globalist agenda. So on what matters should these supranational globalist oligarchies decide? Well, about climate change, about the pandemic, social justice, inequality, etc. which are basically the issues that are part of the dogmas of the globalist agenda.

Thus, this new paradigm seems to start with climate change, since in February 2021 the new book by Bill Gates "How to avoid a climate disaster. The solutions we have and the breakthroughs we need" on climate change and transition to a world that emits less carbon dioxide into the atmosphere through the use of renewable energy was published.

In this way, Klaus Schwap and the rest of the social engineers consider that in order to change the system, it is first necessary to eliminate all the governance structures that currently protect citizens from being regulated by these elites and supranational organizations that aspire to say what is relevant, desirable and true of what is not.

That is why what happened in the United States elections is so important and how Trump and his team of lawyers who denounced that there had been fraud in the

November the 3rd 2020 elections were silenced, because it has really shown people what is being done and what has been going on for a long time. Now we are no longer able to talk freely about the United States elections, we are no longer able to talk freely about Bill Gates' several globalist projects, we are no longer able to talk freely about the Covid-19 virus, neither about the vaccines as long as any questions are raised about the official version, which by the way changes by the minute.

So even if we would like the local communities to be able to make decisions out of the box of the globalist dictatorship, then we find that there are no relevant matters that local communities may identify as of their own competence to work in order to solve those problems.

Thus, the globalist dictatorship suppresses the ability to decide for themselves not only to individuals but also to countries, with the ultimate goal of turning these nations into mere protectorates.

And furthermore, as the globalist oligarchies know that the State has a limited capacity, then effectively the States decide to have the large corporations on their side, to which the money from the global economic expansion that emanates from the central banks also reaches, which in turn is received first by the States.

Then these multinationals will make their decisions leaving aside the will of the shareholders and working to follow the guidelines of a group of enlightened people who determine at all times what should be done, which is a technocratic fascism.

And if a politician or a businessman does not publicly declare the official truth promoted by globalist entities, he is thrown out of the presidency of the United States as it happened with Donald Trump through the great conspiracy and electoral fraud. So not only should there be no dissident politicians or businessmen, but also the globalist elites do not want dissident politicians to be able to be voted, nor to create revolutions against globalist policies and measures.

In this way the globalist entities create global problems such as the increase in state debt through continuous monetary expansion and then propose and impose global solutions themselves.

In fact, the global planning of society always ends in chaos, hunger and destruction, and for this global planning to take place first, it is necessary to end the old paradigms as the globalist entities say. But possibly the globalist oligarchies also think that indeed shock or chaos is what allows them to build everything anew, since they have had intellectuals such as the writer Naomi Klein who has served this work of manipulative intellectualism with her famous book " The shock doctrine".

In this book by Naomi Klein there are some analyzes that reflect well the reality but also she blames the economic market for almost everything that is happening now, whilst the market is not the culprit of the current situation, since the continuous monetary expansion and the exponential growth of the States that has happened in the last decades has nothing to do with the free market but with an intervened market.

Thus, the global financial elites want large corporations to use part of that power of the States to hold their clients captive, being simply taxpayers and consumers but not people who may claim their rights, and this they aim to achieve with wars or pandemics.

The new pandemic: the cyber pandemic

The World Economic Forum is promoting at high speed after the Covid-19 pandemic the concept of cyber pandemic, which will possibly be the new threat after the Covid-19 pandemic. Thus, today's society's high dependence on technology makes societies more vulnerable and the social engineers of the global elite have found a perfect enemy to justify population control.

The World Economic Forum bases its strategy on the search for continuous threats that justify the social engineering measures that they propose, measures that have been in the making for a long time and that end up reducing the sovereignty of nations and creating decision-making spaces where democracy disappears in favor of the desire of an oligarchy that imposes their supranational agenda.

Thus, the concept of cyber pandemic is more topical than ever due to the cyberattacks that have affected the very same company Microsoft, which has suffered a massive hack of its servers in early March 2021, which has affected its customers in all over the world, even threatening the national security of the United States and of almost all the countries in the world, since most of the countries are Microsoft customers.

This cyberattack has been so alarming that even the White House has had to react and act because according to the United States National Security Agency the attack has been active for more than a week and infectious disease laboratories, legal firms, universities, defense contractors, data analytics centers and NGOs have also been affected.

But there have also been other cyberattacks such as the one on the Silicon Valley startup Verkada Inc., on whose servers it has the data of 150,000 surveillance cameras, obtaining access to transmissions from hospitals, companies, police departments, prisons, schools, etc. Among the companies affected we find Tesla, which is the jewel of the crown of the richest man in the world today, Elon Musk, whose company aspires to be one of the new axes of this world and of the post-Covidian normal (post Covid-19 normality).

In addition, these cyberattacks affected the IT provider Cloudfare and SolarWinds in December 2020. SolarWinds being a supplier to several agencies in the United States and to multiple Big Tech companies (large technological companies) such as Microsoft,

Ford, Mastercard, Nestle, Harvard University and as many as 425 of the 500 companies on the Fortune magazine's list.

These cyberattacks have even been published by media such as the New York Times, which is an official media which also promotes the globalist agenda, but nevertheless many people have not been aware of it.

Precisely the New York Times is the official source according to the Alliance for the verification of the truth of the news from its very origin to its destination, led by Microsoft itself and which we will talk about in another chapter of this book.

So in the second week of March 2021 there was also a fire in the data center of a French company called OVH, which is one of the most important web hosting providers in the world and which has had important consequences such as digital blackouts and problems in different services. Two of these centers have been almost completely destroyed, affecting encryption tools and cryptocurrency exchanges as many people who happen to buy Bitcoin what they really do is to change it in an exchange house or exchange which saves private customer cryptocurrency keys. In this manner the private key is held by the exchange itself and thus those Bitcoins can be stolen as we saw in a previous chapter on bitcoin and digital currencies. In fact cryptocurrency exchanges do not like to say that Bitcoins can be stolen but there is some degree of possibility about it. So in fact, the only way to prevent the private key from being stolen is to have it written down or printed on a physical paper, that is, through a totally analog way, which is a total paradox in a digital world.

In fact, the conflict regarding the theft of Bitcoin has come because there are video game players who have lost their games which they had been playing for years and paid with bitcoins.

Just as we were saying this OVH company is run by the Klaba family, which is based in France and whose president, Henryk Klaba, was indicted by the judge "De la Mata" of the Spanish National Court and known for erasing client files from the "Idental" dental clinics in Spain, whose fraud affected thousands of clients.

Thus, OVH is financed by KKR, which is one of the large investment funds that has many interests in Spain, and by Tower Group, which is a spin-off of George Soros' investment fund, which in February 2021 signed an agreement with the French company Capgemini to help with data hosting, which happens to be also the company chosen without any public auction or competition in Spain to keep the Covid-19 vaccination registry.

In fact, these consulting companies like Accenture, Capgemini, Ernst & Young, Deloitte, PwC, KPMG, etc. are most of the time the only ones that happen to be paid and to be present in this type of projects. Thus, these consulting companies earn money keeping the record of Covid-19 vaccinations or reporting on rescue funds, as it is the case with the so-called "Next Generation EU", whose report is being carried out by the consulting firm PricewaterhouseCoopers, PwC.

In addition, the OVH servers hosted a part of the WikiLeaks files, which are the documents published by Julian Assange, and also had part of the information of Edward Snowden, who is an American technology consultant, informant, former employee of the Central Agency of Intelligence (CIA) and the National Security Agency (NSA). Thus, Snowden himself said that this company was among the objectives of the intelligence alliance called "Five Eyes", which are the famous 5 Eyes that are made up of the United States, the United Kingdom, Canada, Australia and New Zealand.

Moreover OVH is going to go public shortly in competition with Google and Amazon.

In fact, the database of the Spanish Public Service of State Employment was also apparently hacked in early March 2021 requiring the intervention of the Spanish intelligence services, whose cyberattack appears to have been perpetrated by three Russian groups using a ransomware virus (computer virus programmed to request a monetary ransom in exchange for being removed) called "ryuk". These groups apparently perpetrated a double cyber attack as they asked for money in order to remove the virus and also kept part of the documentation, later posting it on the dark web to show that they had accessed it.

All these cyberattacks have occurred in a matter of days and have been massively exposed in the mainstream media outlets, which is rather strange because normally these events are hidden as they generate fear and distrust in new technologies, and therefore they go against the message of the globalist agenda that we must depend more on new technologies.

So why do large agencies and media help to generate this state of permanent alert and fear?.

They do so by reporting the number of people infected and died by the Covid-19 virus all the time, by reporting the possibility of nuclear attacks, as the British magazine "The Economist" recently did with the cover of its issue published on January the 30th 2020 saying: "Who will go nuclear next?". They also introduce fear with the idea of a supposed climate emergency, as for example Bill Gates has done with the publication of the book that we discussed earlier, which is based on the political and economic interests that are grouped mainly around the World Economic Forum, whose president Klaus Schwab, has been obsessed with the concept of the Fourth Industrial Revolution for years, which in June 2020, three months after the Covid-19 pandemic was decreed, recorded a video statement saying this:

"We all know it but we still do not pay enough attention to the terrifying scenario that would occur after a comprehensive cyberattack that would cause the cut of supply and energy transport, affecting hospital services and society as a whole. The Covid-19 crisis will then be seen as a small disturbance compared to a large cyberattack. We must use the Covid crisis as a temporary opportunity to reflect on the lessons that the cybersecurity community can provide us to prepare for a potential cyber pandemic. "

So as we see Klaus Schwab is talking about how we must prepare for a global cyber pandemic when we have not yet finished with the Covid pandemic. Is it that the Covid pandemic has not been enough? Is it that perhaps they need to update the threats to keep us in tension?.

In fact with the generating of tension there will always be powerful and lucky people who will win on this regard, and it is quite obvious that after more than a year with the Covid pandemic there is indeed a strategy to instill fear in the population, as if the magnates of the World Economic Forum and the promoters of the globalist agenda dreaded that the population could lose the fear of contagions and deaths from Covid-19.

In this way we are effectively facing the end of an economic and political model and it seems that the people who held the power are nervous and worried about losing it and want to keep it at all costs.

In this way, the World Economic Forum or popularly known as the Davos Forum has been spreading this type of message for some time and the Covid-19 has precisely been an element to give impetus to this type of ideas.

In this way the video we just talked about of the president of the World Economic Forum, Klaus Schwab, is one of many. In the same way we have other videos of the managing director of the World Economic Forum, Jeremy Jurgens, insisting on the idea that we are at the door of another pandemic, also stating that there will be another even more significant crisis, faster and with a greater impact than the Covid-19 one. Therefore it is logical to wonder whether they are warning, threatening or scaring us or all three options together so that we accept what they are offering us.

So it seems that the tycoons who promote the globalist agenda and specifically the tycoons of the World Economic Forum in their communications seek to keep the world population terrified.

But the truth is that there are always going to be cyberattacks and computer vulnerabilities, whether cybersecurity is managed at local or national levels, or as the moguls of the globalist agenda would like it to be, that is at a global supranational level.

Thus, it is true that with the Covid-19 pandemic there has been a greater technological dependence, which precisely globalist entities such as the World Economic Forum have been asking for a long time, which they have also been designing it for a long time. Thus, it would be a plan to exchange our freedom for greater security, but in which the population ultimately loses both freedom and security.

In this way, the cyber pandemic predicted by the World Economic Forum would be the next phase of the Great Reset. Some people say that it would be the fourth phase of the Great Reset that Klaus Schwap tells in his book "Covid-19. The Great Reset ". In this way the acceleration of technological dependence produced by the limitation in mobility due to the restrictions imposed by the Covid-19 pandemic has also produced an increase in cyberattacks, what Klaus Schwap also explains in the book mentioned above, which would be a modern version of the ancient nuclear threat or the Islamic terrorist threat.

So it is significant they are not only making us afraid but we are also being attacked at the same time

In addition, these supranational magnates use the semantic in order to sow fear, so one of the articles that was published in the World Economic Forum in February 2021 is illustrated with a syringe with the title "How to vaccinate your organization against a cyber pandemic ". But what do vaccines have to do with cyber pandemics?. So it is true that many of the computer attacks are carried out through programs called viruses, but it seems that there is a clear intention to continue watering the seed of fear planted with the Covid-19.

In this way, an attempt is made to relate a virus to a computer cyberattack, as other times the promoters of the globalist agenda relate concepts that in theory have nothing to do with a pandemic, for example relating the pandemic with climate change, the conquest of space with a gender perspective, which shows that the magnates of this agenda mix dogmas, concepts and objectives of the globalist agenda in their messages.

The idea that there is a clear intention to feed the seed of fear that began with the constant information about the number of infections and deaths from Covid-19 by the media, becomes a reality when we verify that there is a program promoted by the agenda of the World Economic Forum called Cyber Polygon.

Broadly speaking, Cyber Polygon is one of those war games that social engineers and the military-industrial complex like so much, which also the Big Tech (large technology companies) have joined. This Cyber Polygon program is reminiscent of the Event 201, that is on the website of the John Hopkins University, because it is who organized it, being the John Hopkins University deep state in its purest form, along with the Bill and Melinda Gates Foundation and the World Economic Forum itself.

All the information about the Event 201 is available on the internet and through this event a war game or simulation was played in the fall of 2019, in which the arrival of a pandemic caused by a coronavirus was precisely considered.

In fact only two months later, news about a new Wuhan virus, the Covid-19, would begin to be heard and since so little time had passed since the Event 201 was held, the John Hopkins University published a statement saying that the coincidence of the simulation of the Event 201 with the Covid-19 pandemic was pure chance.

The truth is that it is hard to believe that this coincidence is due to pure chance, but rather that the Covid-19 is the real-life implementation of the Event 201. In this way just three months after the central scenario of this simulation exercise of a pandemic caused by a coronavirus the theoretical exercise came true. In the case of the Cyber Polygon event, what is simulated is a global cyberattack that will spread faster and further than any biological virus, which is just what the World Economic Forum is saying. On this scenario that has been proposed the reproduction rate of this cyberattack is ten times higher than that of the Covid-19.

This cyber pandemic would affect, in addition to basic services, computer data and electricity supply in hospitals, and therefore if there is a lack of power in hospitals, for example all the people that are using respirators due to the Covid-19 virus would die.

In this way, the cyber pandemic would also affect the security and defense infrastructures of the people themselves, who in the future may be connected by electronic devices, which is known as the internet of bodies, which is a concept that arises from the transhumanism project which I explained in the first part of this book.

In fact, the first edition of the Cyber Polygon was held in the middle of the year 2020, that is, there has already been a previous edition. And so precisely since the first edition of the Cyber Polygon was held in the spring of 2020, we have seen an increase in cyberattacks, although fortunately there has not been a global cyberattack among other reasons because the way they put it does not seem a credible or real scenario.

The next edition of the Cyber Polygon will be on July the 9th 2021. In the 2020 edition one of the most prominent speakers was Vladimir Vetrov, son of the Russian spy Vladimir Alexandrovich Vetrov, who ended up as a double agent during the World War II, and who spoke about misinformation and fake news.

As the World Economic Forum says on its website, the 2021 interventions will focus on the safe development of technological ecosystems. This concept of "safe development of technological ecosystems" is going to be heard very often, spreading the idea that many of the technological ecosystems are accelerating with the global digitization, whislt more and people, companies and countries are increasingly interconnected. So the safety of each element is the key to guarantee the sustainability of the entire system.

In the Cyber Polygon what they do is showing their skills to mitigate an attack directed at the supply chain of a corporate ecosystem in real time and thus increase resilience. This Cyber Polygon scenario is what is happening now and it is what has happened with Microsoft and the web hosting company OVHcloud.

So when we enter the World Economic Forum website, the Cyber Polygon has its own space within the World Economic Forum website and on the right-hand side of the header shows up the main partners of the project

The first partner of the Cyber Polygon happens to be again the "Banco de Santander", that seemingly gets involved in these globalist projects to continue surviving.

Precisely the main shareholder of Banco Santander is the largest investment fund in the world, Black Rock, being also Banco Santander one of the greatest promoters of the globalist 2030 Agenda in Spain, which promotes the sustainable development type of goals along with all of the other globalist ideas like climate change, massive immigration, gender equality policies, etc.

Other partners of the Cyber Polygon event are the VISA card company, the Russian news agency Tass, the Russian bank Sberbank, which is a bank that everyone believes is part of the Russian government itself. In this way we may wonder whether this Russian bank is a partner of the Cyber Polygon just to extract information from it or for what other reason.

Therefore everyone seems to be simulating an apocalyptic cyberattack, and it seems that this idea of a technological blackout as a consequence of an attack on basic systems is a resource. In other words, it is a resource that many supposed informants have been using for a long time and that was also included in that calendar of events that became popular within the QAnon (Q) movement. One of the stages of the supposed awakening of humanity that the followers of this movement expected was a massive "blackout", which would leave people without telecommunication services and with serious problems of access to energy and food.

In this way, once again there is an argumentative relationship between the supposedly dissident movements and the globalist architects. So if the messages are the same, even if they temporarily do not coincide, we must ask ourselves if the globalist movements and these dissident movements are not organized by people from the same side.

The concept of the Great Reset is not from the World Economic Forum, since this concept arises many years ago in that environment of supposedly dissident movements to return to the gold standard, because capitalism was supposed to be mortally wounded, or rather the monetary system is mortally wounded and has taken capitalism down with it, whilst now we are in that phase of technocratic corporatism.

Therefore there may be dissident movements that are rowing in the same direction as the visible drivers of the globalist agenda, and so there may even be globalist agendas and sub-agendas.

But today the problem is that the media outlets have been reporting publicly and massively for months with articles, videos, reports, etc. that suggest that this terrifying scenario could be real. Thus, the official New Yorker magazine says that this scenario is already happening and real, as stated in an article that is published and accessible to everyone on the internet of February the 1st 2021 entitled "The next cyberattack is already under way", in which it explains that there is a fever for gold and digital weapons and that the infrastructure that allows us to do our daily lives has never been more vulnerable.

So the message of fear is being supported by the companies affected by the cyberattacks themselves. In this way the Edison International group, whose activity is the energy supply and which is based in California, has published an article signed by one of its top executives, in which assures that the United States energy network has prevented millions of cyberattacks in 2020. Also in this article it is said that they are working 24 hours a day and 7 days a week, but the strange thing is that with a global pandemic still going on fears about the electricity supply are being discussed in the United States.

Therefore these type of messages are not accidental, because although it is evident that infrastructures must be protected from attacks of all kinds and cyberattacks are happening more and more often every day, the truth is that everything indicates that the people are being prepared to assume as normal what really is not. That is the "new normal" in which fear is a common factor.

The concept of global fear has been in the reports of defense departments and agencies for many years. Thus, it is not a new concept nor is it by chance that everyone has started to use it at the same time, because in the end there are certain news agencies that are the ones that have most of the oligopoly of the media, and what these news agencies report using new terms then later it is replicated by other media outlets. However there are other terms that might be even more useful, like the Great Seclusion that was used once by the International Monetary Fund and was never used again.

In this way, the Great Seclusion defines the present crisis better than the term "the Covid crisis", since in fact it is the crisis produced by the seclusion or the restrictions imposed by the governments. A crisis in which we know that we cannot go out on the streets as we would like to, that we cannot open our businesses as we would like to, so businesses end up going bankrupt because of the restrictions imposed and not because of the Covid-19 virus.

In addition, to add more fuel to the fire, it turns out that one of Israel's top cybersecurity officials, Yigal Unna, assured in 2020 that Iran is already carrying out attacks on the water infrastructure of the country of Israel and that in May 2020, one month before the Cyber Polygon event in 2020 took place, was about to compromise the water supply of the Israeli citizens. He talks about how we are on the verge of a cyber winter. It would be the cybernetic "Winter is coming", referring to the first episode of the popular series Game of Thrones. In this way when these guys responsible for cybersecurity pose this scenario, it is possible that they themselves will do the same, because this Israeli officer works in the 8200 unit of Israel's intelligence, which is a unit that has a long history of electronic espionage against the United States, while it appears that the United States National Security Agency has been responsible for several devastating attacks such as the Stuxnet virus, which damaged Iran's nuclear program precisely. In other words, Yigal Unna is telling us that the Iranians are trying to attack their infrastructures but that Israel is going to fight back with other weapons. So as it seems they are talking about and creating this water supply problem because they are using other weapons, and specifically a weapon that is able to leave a population without water, as in this case would happen against Iran. By the way this military action carried out by Israeli intelligence is a typical case of what in cybersecurity is called zero-day attacks. Zero-day is a term that refers to a technology problem that is unknown if we are on zero-day because a solution to that problem is not yet known. It can then refer to system software vulnerabilities such as viruses, worms, malware (includes different types of malicious software) and to attacks that exploit those back doors and their vulnerabilities. One of those malware is the one that has attacked Microsoft, which happens to be the company that aspires to create a global census which will prove whether people are vaccinated or not, whether we will be able to go from one country to another or not, whether we will have the right to basic services or not. Thus Microsoft is one of those who has an important back door, since Microsoft computers and networks are not controlled by anyone.

Besides in the end this Stuxnet computer worm became famous for attacking the digital and computer equipment that controls the production of enriched uranium, which is the uranium used to make nuclear weapons.

Anyhow it seems quite obvious that the Israeli deep state may be one of the beneficiaries of the Great Reset like any other deep state in the world. In fact, in Israel they have already vaccinated most of the population and a good part of the population is already testing the control systems that Covid passports represent, while the country's technological industry is growing very fast .In this way the magazine "Times" of Israel already stated in 2019 that Israeli companies, many of them technology startups, are prepared to lead the fourth industrial revolution, which is the fourth industrial revolution sponsored by Klaus Schwab, which is the title of one of his books.

It is also curious that Joe Biden himself has referred several times to the arrival of a dark winter, known as Dark Winter, referring to the impact of the coronavirus pandemic. There is a lot of talking about Dark Winter in a figurative sense because we are going to a stage in which we are going to be very bad, due to the crisis that Covid-19 has caused, and Biden suggests that the necessary measures must be taken to stop the threat with the invaluable collaboration of the military industrial complex and the Big

Tech (large technology companies), that are becoming more and more powerful and that work together on making control, tracking and monitoring methods.

Thus, it seems clear that when the fear of contagions and deaths from Covid-19 seems to be extinguished, they want to create fear for some other reason. Significantly Google and Apple have already submitted technological proposals to the British Department of Health for control and monitoring purposes testing drugs with humans, which have been rejected for violating fundamental human rights.

So It also turns out that Dark Winter was the name of an operation similar to the Event 201 and to Cyber Polygon, a war game that took place in June 2001 months before the attack on the Twin Towers and that simulated a worldwide smallpox attack, which was also organized by the John Hopkins University, which as we have already said it is part of the USA Deep State, understanding as Deep State to the administration that controls the government of a country in the shadow.

In this way here are times when the actions and movements of the elite do not seem to make much sense, but in this case the incentive for this campaign of fear is evident, which would be social control and the assault on fundamental rights and freedoms. So the case of Australia is a good example as its government in 2018, before the arrival of the Covid pandemic, approved a legislative package that allows access to citizens' communications indiscriminately. This legislative package was approved by consensus between the two main parties of the country, although at the beginning there was one of the parties that could be identified a little bit with the British Labor party which opposed to it, although ultimately signed on to such an extent that the Australian government is empowered to force local and international providers, including technological giants like Facebook, WhatsApp, etc. and several other companies to remove electronic protections, hide undercover operations from government agencies, and help with the access to devices or services. And furthermore, Australian authorities can require by law that all such requests may be kept secret, which happens in a similar way with the USA Patriot Act Law and many other laws in other nations.

So the idea that they spy and totally control us inside of the "smart cities" is also an idea of the globalist agenda, since we would depend on the technology with sensors and devices that make up the Internet of Things (IoT for its acronym in English). Thus, as Klaus Schwab said in his book "Covid-19: The Great Reset", for example, with smart toilets, automatic urine tests are sent to doctors, and if the urine tests are not correct, the doctors may come to look for people in their homes, as it could happen in any movie with a dystopian future, whilst it is not clear that these doctors would bring the people back home later.

This dystopia of the future is quite reminiscent of what happened at the beginning of the pandemic in China, where people were dragged down the street if they did not put on a mask, did not want to take the Covid-19 test or tested positive to it.

Thus, one threat is replaced by another, and now the Soviet threat of the Cold War has been replaced by the Chinese threat, while before the arrival of the Covid-19 pandemic the global threat was Islamic terrorism.

All these threats vary depending on their presence in the media and depending on who is the president in the USA White House, and now once the great seclusion for the Covid-19 is taking place, the use of technology and the new enemy emerge, who can usually be identified as a hacker, being most of the time Russian or Chinese. However people do not seem to realize that all governments use the technology to commit misdeeds and to defend themselves against those committed by others. So what happens in the end is that the power of the globalist technocracies increases little by little, which is the threat that nobody talks about because the media is already in charge of diverting our attention in this regard.

Thus, the threat is not that Microsoft will get a security hole or that they will enter their physical databases and steal them, but the real problem is that there is a technocracy that tells us that in order for those cyberattacks not to happen again against Microsoft, then we have to hand over all of our personal data to them and that they will be in charge of managing our entire lives.

So as this campaign is executed through fear of an external enemy, taking advantage of the fact that citizens have suffered a global brainwashing, now the globalist technocracy is stepping on the accelerator to carry out its agenda even further.

All this to advance in the creation of a technocratic corporatist super state that is the real threat, while we are told that this global corporatist state is the one that will be able to solve global threats. Fortunately the problem that globalist social engineers have is that there are many heavyweights at their meeting tables and each one has their own interests outside of the globalist agenda, which consequently makes the implementation of this globalist agenda to be delayed.

In other words, in the meetings of globalist entities such as the World Economic Forum, the Council for Inclusive Capitalism, the G30, etc. there are many people at the table who want their share of the cut.

In fact it seems that between these globalist masters there is not a total agreement but there are general lines, and then they position themselves to see how to take advantage of this agenda against the personal interests of the other globalist oligarchs.

6

Bill Gates's World: Covid-19, Vaccines, Microchips, and Global Warming

Bill Gates is a planner and a social engineer and what everyone knows is that he has been a successful computer scientist, founder of the Microsoft company, and that he is an impressive mathematician who spends most of his day thinking, nibbling on a pencil or his glasses, which is like a little tic that he has. So he seems to be the perfect man because he is a social planning engineer who considers himself to be above the rest and he is also a billionaire and one of the richest men in the world. In a famous TED Talk that Bill Gates gave in 2015, he effectively anticipated that the great risk to humanity would not come from any war but from a pandemic. He literally said that the next big risk will not be missiles but microbes.

And then it is logical to wonder whether Bill Gates is a prophet because he guesses or because he participates in the decision-making that makes things happen later or to happen as they do it today. Obviously, the Bill and Melinda Gates Foundation and the Gavi Global Vaccination Alliance, of which the Bill and Melinda Gates Foundation are one of the founders and main sponsors, have taken positions in the pharmaceutical sector in an important way.

In fact, Bill Gates in the United States is asked many things regularly, either about medicine or about climate change, that is, about questions in which he does not have to have a greater preparation than a doctor, for example, who is working in a hospital or a knowledge greater than a physicist specialized in climatology in the case of climate change.

So Bill Gates probably has a knowledge of medicine that is not much better than that of a willful amateur but basically what happens is that the weight that he has in the Big Pharma industry is immense, whereas in the field of the vaccines that weight is huge.

By the way there is a rumor that has become more and more widespread in Washington D.C. for a long time which is that the coronavirus is not something only created in the laboratory but is also linked to the Big Pharma (large pharmaceutical companies). And there are those who point out in the United States that the Covid-19 virus has also been released to compensate for the economic losses suffered by the Big Pharma (large pharmaceutical companies) since the presidency of Barak Obama with The Affordable Care Act or popularly known as Obama Care, that is, with the law to extend health coverage to more groups of people, especially the most vulnerable such as those with lower incomes or the elderly. In this way with the Covid-19 virus, they had an open path to produce and sell vaccines with which to do business.

But going back again to the Great Reset it is not about just 8, 9 or 10 meeting in a room and that's it, but rather we are talking about many rooms talking about many rooms, many tables, in which they also discuss at those tables to see who has more power among different families and people of different ideologies, and there are also blood families who are sitting at those tables. And then there are a series of characters who happen to be more in the public arena, who these elites want to be there as well.

In this way, with the subject of vaccines, what has been done lately is to try to demonize this Covid-19 vaccine with alternative theories or conspiracy theories so that in this way everyone loses the fear of getting the vaccine, since in general when we hear that a news or event has been crossed out or branded as conspiranoic (that comes from a conspiracy theory), this usually creates the opposite effect and people tend to lose the fear they had about it. In fact, Bill Gates's main objective is that everyone gets vaccinated as he indicated in an interview in early 2021 with CNBC and has even made calculations of how much it would cost for all of us to get vaccinated. He says that it would take just over $ 40 million to immunize the entire world, though of course he is expecting taxpayers to pay for the vaccines.

So what Bill Gates said at the beginning of 2021 is that the first 6 months of this year would be the worst of the pandemic, which is something that some of us have been saying for a long time. In addition, Bill Gates knows how many people are going to die in the United States until April 1, 2021, which he said would be 200,000 people according to a figure made by a metric institute. Bill Gates right now is fundamentally dedicated through the Bill and Melinda Gates Foundation to an institute of metrics with which he performs these social analyzes that serve every engineer or planner to be able to justify that what he is doing is done because science says so, as in the same way calculations were made in his day to put people in concentration camps also theoretically based on science.

In addition, in regards to the the Gavi Vaccination Alliance, which is in charge of vaccinating half of the planet and of manufacturing the vaccines, Bill Gates himself also has a personal interest. However, Bill Gates has a blog called "Gates' notes" and he already said that the first week of 2021 was not going to be as bad as 2020, that the worst would be the month of January, and then everything would be fine because we are all going to get vaccinated, so it seems that someone has caught his attention and told him to stop scaring people so that people could get the vaccine.

But regarding vaccines, although they should not be mandatory, it seems that we will have to be vaccinated to even access shopping centers, enter stores or travel and that they will not leave us much of a choice whether or not getting vaccinated.

Obviously, the elderly and those at risk of having immune, heart or serious diseases would pay off themselves for the cost of the vaccines, but the Global Vaccination Alliance, GAVI, and Bill Gates want everyone to be vaccinated despite the multitude of adverse effects that are causing Covid-19 vaccines such as the Pfizer or especially the AstraZeneca Covid-19 vaccine, whose administration has been stopped in several countries. In this way we are not talking about starting with some people and then if things are going well continuing with another age group, but Bill Gates wants the entire planet to be vaccinated.

As in the world we are about almost 8,000 million people and then with some vaccines like Pfizer's people are supposed to get two doses, and then every year people will have to be vaccinated again, so these pharmaceutical companies are going to make astronomical profits which they can`t let go.

So vaccinating most the world's population would be another way to get the money out of the public budgets of the nations to pay for the vaccines, which, as with the public debt of the nations, will end up being paid by the middle classes with their taxes. In fact, the nations will go into even more debt to buy these vaccines that in the end the poor taxpayers will pay with their taxes, contrary to what they want us to believe that these vaccines are paid by pharmaceutical companies or States and that they are free of cost.

In fact, in many underdeveloped countries of the world, including Latin American countries and Spain itself, it has happened constantly in the last decades that the elites at the top steal from the middle classes blatantly, but they do it through the public budget and then they give out little crumbs to these middle and lower classes because there are elections every four years and they want to keep the middle and lower classes happy so that they may continue voting for the politicians who are in power.

In this way, the theory of dangerous climate change, known as global warming, is one of many instruments used to justify policies to get money out of the public budget of the States, theories that are widely and constantly published by the government-related media.

That is why when the same messages are transmitted in all the television channels, in all official media outlets and social platforms, then it is necessary to ask ourselves what is really happening and whether they are informing us well or on the contrary they are informing us according to what they want us to hear and think about.

Indeed, there is an economic interest for everyone to get vaccinated to which an important incentive is added, and that is that if the Great Reset is characterized by something, it is that we are talking about something more than money but also shepherding the herd playing games of being God.

In this way, the intelligence services of consulting companies are dedicating themselves, especially in the Covid-19 plandemic (planned pandemic), to mixing truths with lies in order to discredit any criticism of the single thought system. Thus, Bill Gates himself has been attacked by the most critical people pointing out his supposed objective of implanting a hidden chip in vaccines to control the world population, which is false.

Thus, especially since the beginning of the Covid-19 pandemic, information has increased, but above all misinformation, so that we are even more responsible today for informing ourselves well.

In fact, to misinform and confuse people, some elements that are true are mixed with others that are not, which serves to discredit the critics of the globalist agenda and qualify them as a group of paranoids who take the streets to demonstrate on this regard. This is then the weapon that misinformers use since it is not necessary to shut down an account on social media platforms for example, but it is enough to simply ridicule a person for their ideas, to take the ideas of the dissidents to the extreme or to mix the ideas of the other person with lies for example.

In fact the idea that Bill Gates' vaccines are microchipped comes from a truth, which is from the fact that Bill Gates wants to implant capsules in humans with microchips, but not through Covid-19 vaccines. In this way, there is an ongoing investigation being carried out by the MIT, Massachusetts Institute, which is a totally globalist institution, together with the Rice University in Houston, that regularly collaborate with the Bill and Melinda Gates Foundation in relation to a technology that is called "quantum dot tattoos"," which is a kind of invisible ink that is put into the skin every time someone gets a vaccine, which has already been approved but is not yet operational.

This technology is a new dye that is made of small crystals or nano crystals, which are called quantum dots through a technology that is very similar to that of LEDs. In this way with a mobile device itself, it is passed around the skin and through an infrared light the person is detected by the smartphone as it happens when they mark the cows or as they also mark the prisoners of the concentration camps, which It is intended to be a substitute for the current vaccination cards.

Thus, these supranational globalist entities and oligarchies say that this technology would be of great benefit, but the truth is that there are less developed territories where there are no vaccination cards or digital databases. So the logical solution would be for the governments of these countries themselves to be in charge of those vaccination registries and not global organizations that no one has voted for. It is a technology that would like incorporate most of the data of a person's life. In other words, not only the medical history but for example also the financial history, a project that is promoted by the multinational debit and credit card company Mastercard.

The next step in terms of these quantum dot tattoos is also Bill Gates' project called ID2020, who directly wants to do a global digital census.

Thus, among the objectives of the 2030 Agenda, the United Nations includes as one of the goals to provide legal identity for everything including birth registration through the ID2020 program, in which we find the same globalist companies behind of this project as always, that is the Rockefeller Foundation, Microsoft, the Global Vaccine Alliance, Gavi, Mastercard, organizations dedicated to the use of biometric data, pharmaceutical companies and the UN itself through specifically the "International Computing Center" of the United Nations. In addition, the ID2020 digital identification system is already in the testing phase in Texas, United States.

Thus, the idea is that we will use this digital identity tattooed on our body to access social and health services, because the objective of the Rockefeller Foundation, of Bill Gates and of these globalist elites is first to digitize all the data and introduce it inside our body. Although at first it seemed that the ID2020 identification system would not be necessary because people already go with their mobile device to all places, which contains practically all their personal information. In this regard these oligarchs say that this digital identity is meant to provide them with social services, but in fact it is quite the opposite, that is to have the entire population that lives on the edge of subsistence framed through the aid of the State. And this globalist technocracy also says that this digital identity tattooed on our bodies would serve to execute political rights, such as voting and carrying out economic transactions, a project that is published on the website of the Massachusetts Institute. In addition, this project has been presented in 2017 to the United Nations and in 2019 at the Davos Forum, that is, at the World Economic Forum.

Thus, Bill Gates, who is the main financier or financier of the World Health Organization together with the most important world laboratories, is at the same time in charge or will be together with the historic and powerful Rockefeller Foundation of laying the foundations for the registration and biometric control of the population. Although at the beginning of 2021 a video of "Anonymous", which is a decentralized international activist/hacktivist collective/movement, came out threatening Bill Gates with revealing the supposed true intentions of the ID2020 project which happens to be the only fact that nobody talks about. But perhaps there is another family within this elite that uses Anonymous to attack those who criticize Bill Gates and his projects, because these types of organizations like Anonymous also tend to work for certain purposes.

Thus Bill Gates had a closer relationship with Jeffrey Epstein than he would like to accept, flying in Jeffrey Epstein's private jet, having meetings with both Epstein and his close circle at the Bill and Melinda Gates Foundation. But when this was discovered, what did the misinformers do?. The media published that Bill Gates was on Jeffrey Epstein's island which is false and discredits all information about Bill Gates's relationship with Jeffrey Epstein.

In reality, these mechanisms of misinformation and of discredit are very easy to organize, because once they are released go viral automatically. Thus, there may be serious journalists who are very well informed, but if they also report false news or facts because they have not been able to filter or investigate this news well, then people stop taking these journalists seriously.

Therefore, if journalists do not investigate and confirm the news that they receive and publish it directly, then they also involuntarily become disinformers and become instruments of misinformation.

So continuing with the relationship between Bill Gates and Jeffrey Epstein, which is not discussed in the media, it should also be added that Epstein has been a facilitator of donations from Bill Gates to the Massachusetts Institute of Technology, MIT, which we mentioned earlier, that is to say, Jeffrey Epstein acted as an intermediary and there is no mention of the flights that Bill Gates made on the Lolita Express plane, as this pedophile's plane was known. In fact, Bill Clinton used to take the escorts on this plane itself, which is something that is said in the documentation that judges in the United States have brought to light.

And on the other hand we also have the relationship with Bill Gates' pornography, which is something that has been tried to cover up. The truth is that "The Independent newspaper" published in July 2007 that Gates had bought the majority of the PlanetOut group, which is mainly dedicated to homosexual pornography. And the investment was made through the financial company Cascade Investment, which is also one of the companies controlled by the tycoon. In this way PlanetOut presents itself as the leading community of gays, lesbians, bisexuals and transexuals, organizing cruises for the LGTBIQ + collective, etc. It is not that the LGTBIQ + collective does not have the right to enjoy cruises and a good life, but nobody would imagine that Bill Gates could also support a group that is mainly dedicated to homosexual pornography.

So the truth is not whether Bill Gates wants or does not want to put chips in people through the administration of vaccines for the Covid-19, but the truth is that he wants to promote the use of contraceptive capsules with microchips and quantum dot tattoos. Some of these tattoos may end up being implanted in most nations and may even be interesting for the millennial generation, since it is possible that depending on the mood that we have these tattoos will light up in one color or another for example and even these Quantum dot tattoos may end up being put on people voluntarily because they so desire.

Related to microchips there is already a technology and project of contraceptive pills with microchips that has been published by the Massachusetts Institute of Technology, MIT.

In fact, Bill Gates' family has already been keen on limiting the population on the planet, which is one of the family obsessions, since his father sat on the board of directors of Planned Parenthood, the world's leading abortion organization. By the way, in all the documentaries about Bill Gates, his father appears as the second parent in terms of importance, while the first is his mother.

In this way, if we go to the website of the Bill and Melinda Gates Foundation we will find a company called Microchips Biotech Inc., and in a section of this page entitled "How we work", we see that it is a company dedicated to developing digital birth control pills that are activated by remote control.

Therefore Bill Gates and his associated companies do want to implant microchips, and in fact there are many patents and documents that prove this, on which many people base their theories claiming that they are going to implant microchips in humans.

So even if there are people who deny the fact that they are going to implant microchips, the problem may be that many people may want to have these microchips implanted in them, therefore they are going to ask to have them implanted or even pay to have them implanted, as in a similar way already It is happening in Sweden, where there are already more than 4,000 people who by March 2021 have already had a chip implanted between their thumb and index finger of the size of a grain of rice, with which they can make payments without the need of credit cards, which in turn would be an advantage to avoid contagion of Covid-19 by avoiding contact with credit cards or cash.

In this way, these microchips and quantum dot tattoos will possibly be put on by many people voluntarily because it will make it much easier to do many transactions. This way, it will not be necessary to carry a credit card, carry the plane ticket or medical records. That is, it is supposed to make daily life easier.

What could also happen as a result of the implantation of microchips in human beings is that at a certain moment a microchip theft industry was created. That is, if they know that someone has a microchip, then they remove the microchip and thus taking their money and all their data, which will be similar or even worse to when today our mobile phone is stolen with all our data in it.

But as we have mentioned before, the great obsession of Bill Gates is overpopulation, which is the old and outdated Malthusian idea that population grows much more than resources, while there are other tycoons like Elon Musk or Jack Ma, the co-founder and president of the Alibaba group, who believes that there is going to be a population collapse within the next 20 years. They speak of an accelerating collapse even including the birth data in underdeveloped countries that have higher birth rates. So Gates' obsession is overpopulation, although he hides it a little more now, since it is not the same to say that they want to reduce the planet's population when there is a global pandemic than when there is not.

In this way, the use of microchips in humans is also part of transhumanism, that is, the human being will be able to merge with technology to evolve to a higher stage, but always evolving from the man himself. Thus, this project of transhumanism is also part of the globalist agenda as we saw in the first part of this series, and not only human beings will be connected with the electronic devices around them forming part of the internet of things and transmitting data at all times, may it be health data, location, etc. but the population has also to be reduced, which the globalist oligarchies have been studying for decades how to do it.

However, the thesis that on the contrary what is going to occur is a collapse of the population, since there is more and more elderly population in the world and proportionally fewer new births in order to sustain with their work and activity the expenses and needs of the elderly, it is not a crazy idea but in some cases it is pretty evident. For example, China realized years ago that it needs several hundred million more births than it has because it cannot keep up with the current population growth. And in fact, the enormous flexibility with the law of the only son that there was in China is mainly due to the fear of not having the population growth that they need to reach a hegemonic position in the world.

So it is true that perhaps in Shanghai, in Beijing, in Nanjing or in one of the main Chinese cities we will not find families that have more than one child, but if we go to countryside cities that are immense compared to the Western cities, being also relatively modest Chinese cities and second and third-tier ones in China, we find families that of course have more than one child and there is enormous flexibility from the authorities in this regard because they are aware that they are going to need hundreds of millions of Chinese more to move on.

Furthermore, if we think about the case of many European nations such as Spain, it is unfeasible for them to prosper economically in the long-term future and some countries might even disappear because they have committed suicide demographically speaking. Whilst if we think that these nations are going to be able to maintain all that framework and all the expenses of a growing State just with the work of immigrants coming from Africa, we are probably wrong. In this way, it is no nonsense to say that there are going to be serious demographic problems in different nations of the world, not just in one or two nations but in many more. What happens is that these globalist tycoons like Bill Gates who are obsessed with the reduction of the world population and with the fact that billions of people of the world must disappear, do not want to accept it.

Moreover, the globalist oligarchies wish to make millions of people on the world to disappear but they have to be from the poor social classes and of course not themselves.

So we ask ourselves how a mathematician like Bill Gates who is a super intelligent person and who reads several books per week is defending the thesis of overpopulation and the need to reduce it by billions of people. But if we analyze a little how the Gates Foundation was born and as Bill Gates himself admits, he did it focused on reproductive health, which is a euphemism to say abortion or killing babies in their mothers' wombs, which is basically what reproductive health is about and what his father did, that is, preventing pregnancies and financing abortions while on the board of the Planned Parenthood organization that is primarily engaged in the abortion business.

However, shortly afterwards, the work of the Bill and Melinda Gates Foundation mutated when it realized that in order to prevent the growth of the population of poor countries, what it had to do was improve people's health, since there are many children in those poor countries not only because of religious reasons but fundamentally to guarantee the survival of the family clan. That is, if many children are going to die due to the living conditions in a poor country, it is necessary to have many children so that they may also support their parents when they are old, because in addition, in these countries there is no type of welfare state or pensions.

In this manner the Gates Foundation decided that in addition to having abortions and making birth control pills, they were going to vaccinate the entire population and this is the reason why Bill Gates enters the world of vaccines, knowing that vaccines in many cases have adverse effects among them sterilizing people, which is why vaccines are one extra method for the reduction or the containment of the world population growth.

The sterilization of the population through vaccines has not only happened in Africa but also in Latin America. Therefore it seems quite evident that this risk of sterilization of the population through vaccines was an assumed and also desired risk by those who are in favor of reducing the world's population.

So we must bear in mind that these supranational magnates like Bill Gates see us all as pieces of a chessboard, so whenever someone tells us that they are going to do something for our good it is preferable not to let them. In this way, in the end what we have is Bill and Melinda Gates focusing their efforts and money on mass vaccination of the population through their Foundation, which is precisely the first foundation in the world in capital working in the areas of mass vaccinations, abortion, contraceptives and the development of vaccines, of course with the support of the UN. It is very curious because Melinda Gates says that she is a Catholic and at the same time a believer in contraceptives, which is contradictory, as the current president of the United States, Joe Biden, says that is also a Catholic and a believer in abortion.

In this way given the great importance of these activities carried out by someone like Bill Gates whom no one has voted for and who leads millionaire efforts to direct and control the destinies of millions of people in the world, it is not surprising that many doubted his intentions at the time when he requested that everyone be vaccinated against Covid-19. Furthermore, in many cases the risks associated with the vaccine may outweigh the benefits. So why should we all get vaccinated?

It is also public information that the pharmaceutical companies that have manufactured the Covid-19 vaccines say in their documentation presented to the governments which is also available for public consultation, that they do not know the effects that vaccines may have on fertility. In fact, the pharmaceutical companies themselves recommend not administering these vaccines to pregnant women because they have not yet been tested with them, but nevertheless the governments of many countries decide anyway to administer the vaccines to these pregnant women as well. So who will be responsible for what happens with these vaccines afterwards, especially if governments force people to get vaccinated perhaps not by law but by prohibiting travel if people are not vaccinated, and do not hold a Covid-passport proving that are up to date with the Covid-19 vaccines?.

So it is not about being total anti-vaccines because many vaccines have eradicated diseases such as smallpox in the past, but they are vaccines that take five to ten years to develop, test, and launch on the market. In this way, if the vaccine is indeed a guaranteed vaccine, its years of testing have passed, it is known that it has no side effects, etc. then in these cases the vaccines are positive.

On the other hand regarding the globalist theory of global warming precisely in February 2021, the latest book by Bill Gates was published entitled "How to avoid a climate disaster. The solutions we have and the breakthroughs we need", in which he talks about the energy sources used on the planet today and how to make the transition to a world that barely emits carbon dioxide into the atmosphere using energy sources which are theoretically "clean", what he calls zero emissions, admitting that it is a gigantic and difficult task of collaboration between all nations.

But the reality is that we all get heat thanks to burning gas, burning coal and nuclear energy, being the nuclear energy something that at least Bill Gates does not condemn, since it is true that nuclear energy barely emits carbon dioxide into the atmosphere although it is has been demonized by the accidents at the nuclear power plants of April 26, 1986 in the Chernobyl plant, Ukraine or the most recent leak from the Fukushima nuclear power plant, Japan in May 2011. However it weren't for these energy sources there would be power outages in many nations today.

Thus and for a long time Bill Gates is involved in the lie of global warming in theory produced by greenhouse gases such as the arch-damned carbon dioxide, a theory about which I already spoke in the first part of this book explaining that from a scientific point of view is not proven to be true, but objective scientific evidence shows that carbon dioxide, far from producing any climate disaster, causes more vegetation to grow on the planet, vegetation that in turn absorbs carbon dioxide from the atmosphere in order to grow.

But summarizing Bill Gates in his book "How to avoid a climate disaster" suggests some concrete steps that people, governments and companies should take to achieve zero emissions by 2050, with a medium-term goal of reducing emissions considerably by 2030, which is raised by the World Economic Forum through the Agenda 2030. In this way Bill Gates explains to us how others have to live because he is allegedly the smartest of all, he is good and wants to help people because the rest do not find out. Therefore the problem here is not that Gates writes a book stating that it is necessary to make the energy transition in theory to save the planet from a climate disaster but that many people take what Bill Gates says as a valid scientific reference.

In addition, Bill Gates has been working in Sweden on the Scopex project (Stratospheric Controlled Disturbance Experiment) carried out by scientists from Harvard University to cover the sun by releasing tons of non-toxic calcium carbonate from aerostatic balloons to the atmosphere in order to reflect sunlight and thus cooling the planet. Fortunately, the authorities of the Swedish country have denied the authorization of this project in the first week of April 2021 because the scientific community is divided regarding the need and adverse effects of solar geoengineering.

This fact reminds us of an episode of The Simpsons that seems to have predicted like other times what would happen in the future, being in this case with Bill Gates' Scopex project. So in this episode of the Simpsons they also try to cover the sun directly to stop climate change.

According to the environmentalists themselves, the Scopex project is outrageous, but in any case it is an official project that can be found in publications from the Reuters news agency, for example. So it seems again that some humans and in this case Bill Gates have believed themselves to be gods and the truth is that we have already done very badly believing ourselves gods in the past, as it happened at the beginning in which the devil tempted and deceived the first couple of humans , Adam and Eve, who appear in the story of the first book of the bible, Genesis chapter 3, specifically telling them that if they ate the fruit of the tree of life that God forbade them to eat, they would be like gods knowing good and evil. Then Eve and Adam ate of this fruit and knew good and evil but were not like gods, but became humans fallen by sin.

In addition, Bill Gates also has interests in the agri-food industry, which is why he has started to buy lands in the United States, being today the main landowner of land in this country. Moreover he has been buying genetically modified seed banks for a long time, that is genetically modified seeds manufactured by the Monsanto company together with the multinational pharmaceutical company Bayer. So in the end, the yields of the crops in these areas will be affected since these transgenic seeds can only be used once and do not allow a second generation of plants, crops or fruit trees to be born. This does modify the living conditions of the human being without a doubt.

But in fact the project of releasing calcium carbonate into the atmosphere to cool the atmosphere or any other project that Bill Gates supports, he always does it with the purpose of theoretically avoiding a greater evil, but has Bill Gates really considered the unknown potential adverse effects that may occur if calcium carbonate is released into the atmosphere?.

For these reasons there are doubts about the intentions of Bill Gates, doubts that do not appear in the mainstream media. The famous medical journal "The Lancet" has become very popular in 2021 but ten years ago they did an analysis of the Bill and Melinda Gates Foundation, in which they made a criticism of this Foundation saying negative things about it, accusing the Foundation of a lack of transparency, of spending the money on projects that later did not have the result that was proposed at the beginning. The Lancet also stated that the Foundation was being used as a kind of money washer. And basically what "The Lancet" was saying is that most of the key contributors to global health, whether they may be governments, pharmaceutical companies, healthcare companies or insurance companies have a relationship in one way or another with the Gates Foundation, either through some type of financing agreement or through third-party shell companies. So all these partners of the Gates

Foundation are also their clients. So it is quite well-known that the Bill and Melinda Gates Foundation donates a lot of money to the World Health Organization, which the Foundation later gets it back. In fact, in general all the foundations donate money that they later recover. Thus, for example, the Soros Foundation has financed part of the independence movement in Catalonia, but at a certain point the Soros foundations received money from the Catalan budget as well, and also it is known that they donate a lot money to the World Health Organization as well that the Soros Foundation later recovers.

Summarizing, these foundations put money for these causes but later on they recover it multiplied, for which we just have to keep track of the money if we are interested in finding out.

But one of the biggest problems is that in the end the decisions that someone like Bill Gates makes in an office end up being filtered to society in different strata and through different mechanisms in which governments actively participate. That is why it would be necessary to examine where Bill Gates is psychologically speaking, since he has a lot of influence. So we know that one of the works that Bill Gates recommends is the book entitled "Homo Deus. Brief history of tomorrow. " by the Israeli author Yuval Noah Harari, whilst Gates also confesses to having read "Sapiens. From animals to gods" by the same author.

In fact the book "Sapiens. From Animals to Gods " is a novel although the author says that it is a brief history of humanity and there are people who have taken it as a serious historical essay. So for example the movie "2001: A Space Odyssey" is in many ways more serious on an intellectual level than this book.

Also "Sapiens. From Animals to Gods" is one of the reference books by Mark Zuckerberg, founder of Facebook, and of Barack Obama, whilst in his book "Homo Deus. A Brief History of Tomorrow " the author qualifies death as the last obstacle to progress and immortality as the endless project of humanity to aspire to, falling again back into the error, as we have explained before, of the first couple of human beings of history, to which Satan told them that if they ate the fruit of the tree of good and evil of which God told them not to eat, not only would they not die but they would be like God knowing good and evil. In other words, the aspiration to immortality is something that the human being has already aspired to and that separated him from God. However to this day we continue to fall into the same trap as if the devil was repeating this same lie to Bill Gates and the globalist elite over breakfast every morning.

So today this same aspiration to be gods and for immortality is repeated especially with the movement of transhumanism that aims for the evolution of man through the fusion with the technology.

In this way also in the book "Homo Deus. A brief history of tomorrow" appears a fingerprint drawn with electronic circuits, reminiscent of the graphics of the ID2020 project. In the same way Raymond Kurzweil, who is Google's engineering director, has already said in the years 2000-2001 along with his friends from different technological companies that those of us who refuse to take this evolutionary step will be the chimpanzees of the future.

On the other hand Bill Gates in an interview in the Rolling Stone magazine dated March 13, 2014 when asked if he believed in God, he replied that "it makes sense to believe in God, but what decisions we make differently because of it, I don't know." But precisely if we believe in God and we believe that He listens what we say, sees what we do and how we behave with others, believing that God loves human beings, then we make almost all decisions differently in order to love God and the others as God wants us to.

In this sense, George Soros, who has been another visible promoter of the globalist agenda for decades, says that sometimes he feels that he is god, which is the typical diabolical imprint that all these characters have, not because they celebrate black masses, which I'm not sure of, but because the worldview they have is diabolical. In other words, the old idea of "you will be like gods and you will not know death", has again been swallowed bv these globalist magnates, that is the devil's lie as it happened to Adam and Eve.

So all these people are those that share the ideal of the Great Reset, whose spearhead is the famous Forum of Davos that in 2021 meets in Singapore, in which Bill Gates is one of the prominent members as we can see on the Forum's own website. The World Economic Forum sponsors the Great Reset that aspires to implement the globalist agenda taking advantage of the arrival of Covid-19, as expressed by its president Klaus Schwab in his book "Covid-19: The Great Reset". In this way the goal is to use technology to finish with what little is left of capitalism and through social engineering creating a new socialism. So it seems that citizens are only going to aspire to be able to serve politicians and businessmen who are in coalition in power.

Thus the globalist agenda works with a Hegelian dynamic of action-reaction-solution. In other words, these globalist elites create a problem, then the frightened society asks for measures to solve the problem and finally whoever created the problem appears as a hero with the solution to the problem. However, these alleged heroes, contrary to what their propagandists tell us, have no morals, no principles and above all they consider other human beings their enemies, or worse they consider them guinea pigs with whom they can experiment at will. That is why we must be vigilant and we must analyze everything that is happening so that we may also inform those around us. Nor should we forget to investigate and go to the original sources to verify the veracity of the news and of the facts.

 In this way we have people like Bill Gates who happens to go with a bag full of books to any place and his secretary, depending on what he wants to read, puts a kind of books or others in the bag. That is to say, he is a very intelligent person and he is a reading machine. But apart from Gates we have the rest of the globalist elite who are thinking about how to organize our lives, which is not a conspiracy theory but a fact.

Therefore, let's wake up and go a little beyond the reference websites, where they tell us everything very well ordered, where conspiracies have their beginning and their end, where everything makes sense and where everything fits, because surely at some point or with some element they are lying to us.

8

Covid passport and Big Pharma: the business of fear in the new normal

In fact we are already in a dystopian present similar to the dystopian futures of futuristic films in which there has been some natural, nuclear, virological disaster or some great war that has destroyed most of the planet and has eliminated part of humanity. In this way, the governments of the entire planet qualify it as the "new normal" and that includes certain criteria when it comes to reporting, because if it is reported independently not following the official "mainstream" discourse, it is censored in media platforms, that is, they shut down our YouTube channel or delete the publication on Facebook or Twitter for example.

So it is really curious not to say disturbing how the large pharmaceutical laboratories have traditionally been attacked by the political left, even by the official media outlets of mainstream thought and now coincidentally, these pharmaceutical laboratories are defended by all the official media outlets, making it almost impossible to question their performance or good faith, otherwise being censored because of it.

The problem with pharmaceutical companies is not that they make a lot of profits but that they make them illegally, and thus the fundamental reason that has always been used to criticize the pharmaceutical industry is that they made a lot of money illegally, with unethical practices such as the experimentation of medicines and vaccines with people from underdeveloped countries for example.

Because in fact, if multinational companies earn a lot of money in an ethical and legal way, it simply means that they are providing a product or service demanded and needed by the society, which provides adequate results and has a fair quality and price. In fact many diseases such as polio, rubella, measles, etc. have been practically eradicated thanks to vaccines.

As It has been said, the problem is when pharmaceutical companies earn money thanks to the privileges, to the impunity that politicians grant them on behalf of the States, allowing them to earn exorbitant sums of money through deception, coercion, fraud or in some cases even through murder.

All this could be criticized and denounced before the arrival of Covid-19 but it can no longer be done now without suffering the risk of being censored.

In this way and it is official information, the crimes of the pharmaceutical companies before the arrival of Covid-19 were well known because they were talked about in the media outlets and as we know many of them were serious crimes.

Today the multinational pharmaceutical companies that have developed vaccines for Covid-19 such as Pfizer, AstraZeneca, Abbott, Merck, Johnson & Johnson, GlaxoSmithKline, etc. that make up the Big Pharma conglomerate are those that the former president of the United States, Donald Trump, has accused of being part of the deep state, especially after Pfizer was the first pharmaceutical company in developing the vaccine in the West and managing to find the magic formula right after the presidential elections in the United States on November 3, 2020.

Thus, on November 13, 2020, three researchers Denis Arnold, Oscar Jerome Stewart and Tammy Beck published a report in the American medical journal JAMA, compiling all the sanctions imposed on large pharmaceutical companies between 2003 and 2016 in the United States, in which appear the following crimes that were committed by these Big Pharma: price manipulation, conflicts of interest, unapproved clinical uses, facilitation of kickbacks and bribes, etc.

As for unapproved clinical uses, it means experimenting without having permission to experiment like Josef Mengele did, who was a German SS officer who did experiments on people in concentration camps like Auschwitz.

Furthermore, when these pharmaceutical companies sign contracts with a nation that has not signed Human Rights protocols, often in that country they engage in experiments, for example in children's hospitals. In this way, that contract is effectively signed because that State has not signed a single Human Rights protocol, and in this way it does not have to worry about the protection of children or freedom of expression, or about freeing people from becoming guinea pigs. In this way, this country pockets generous amounts from the Big Pharma and engages in experiments with children in a children's hospital. In this way these facts yield enormous benefits to pharmaceutical companies whilst the parents of the poor children are convinced that their children may be cured of the disease that they suffer.

Sometimes experiments and tests are also carried out with drugs and vaccines with people from the opposition of the dictatorial government in power, which is also done in the prisons themselves, along with the use of misleading drug labels or illegal commissions are being received.

As for Africa, in August 2001, the Nigerian government brought the pharmaceutical company Pfizer, which is the first Western pharmaceutical company to produce the vaccine for the Covid-19, to be convicted in a New York court and sentenced for the death of 11 children in clinical trials with the Trovan test, which was an antibiotic intended to combat meningitis.

They had legal action and were convicted because 30 Nigerian families started a trial before a Court in New York asking that the laboratory was convicted. Although in the end the pharmaceutical company Pfizer negotiated with the Nigerian government because otherwise the pharmaceutical company would have incurred in greater sanctions.

So in the end Pfizer ended up paying the Nigerian government and everything was forgotten, but the fact is that several years later in 2005 clinical trials of other drugs such as Tenofovir, which is also an antiviral used against AIDS, were also suspended in Nigeria. Here they were already involved the organization Family Health on behalf of the American laboratory Gilead Sciences, funded by the United States Government and of course by the Bill and Melinda Gates Foundation. So when we see some kind of health intervention in the third world, Bill and Melinda Gates are behind of it most of the time

The tests were suspended in Cameroon also in February 2005, in Cambodia in 2004, but in Thailand, Botswana, Malawi and in Ghana the tests continued. In this way, in many African countries and in developing countries outside this continent, people have served and are used as human guinea pigs, which is reminiscent of John Le Carré's novel, "The constant gardener" that addresses this topic whose plot also occurs in Nigeria.

So when two French scientists said in April 2020, a few weeks after the Covid-19 pandemic was declared, that Covid-19 vaccines had to be tested in Africa, no one was surprised at first. What happens is that now in the technological society in which we are, these statements went viral on social media platforms and the clinical trials that have been carried out in African and underdeveloped countries for decades could not be turned a deaf ear.

On the French television channel LCI, the scientists who made these statements were the director of research of the French Institute of Medical Research, Camille Locht and

Jean-Paul Mira, head of the Intensive Rehabilitation Medicine Services of the Cochin hospital in Paris.

About this type of clinical trials in Africa and in underdeveloped countries on other continents there is a lot of literature written about it, whilst about the fact that the multinational pharmaceutical companies control the World Health Organization most people know about it.

It is also true that many researchers of the official government media who are the promoters of the single thought now, have denounced in the past that the pharmaceutical companies and the World Health Organization make decisions based almost exclusively on the search for profits, although it is true that these media have never talked much about the Bill and Melinda Gates Foundation, which happens to be the WHO's first private funder.

For example, in the case of influenza A, which is the famous H1N1 virus, which was first known as swine flu, the companies, the investors such as Al Gore, who is the former vice president of the United States under the mandate of Bill Clinton, who also promoted fear so that vaccines would be sold, became rich with the selling of this vaccine.

In this way, the World Health Organization changed the criteria to decree what was or was not a pandemic in May 2019, leaving mortality aside and determining a pandemic based on the number of infected people, therefore changing the criteria in order to be able to decree the "influenza A" a pandemic, so that all governments would begin to buy antivirals and vaccines in bulk, vaccines that in turn mostly ended up in landfills and thrown away.

In fact, there is a report from the British Medical Journal, one of the reference medical journals, which says that the World Health Organization concealed the financial links between its experts and the pharmaceutical companies Roche and Glaxo that are the manufacturers of the famous antiviral Relenza, containing Zanamivir.

But the truth is that the World Health Organization, WHO, and the pharmaceutical companies do not hide some facts too much because Joe Biden has appointed Anthony Fauci as the representative of the United States in the WHO, who had always been a worker for the Big Pharma, director of the National Allergy Institute and Infectious Diseases in the United States since 1984, including in the presidency with Donald Trump and after the Covid-19 pandemic was declared. Joe Biden could have put any other US representative at the World Health Organization, who had closer interests with him, but maybe he put Anthony Fauci because he had to return a favor or pay him for his past work at multinational pharmaceutical companies or as a director of the Institute of Allergy and Infectious Diseases.

Thus, for example, the Spanish journalist Iñaki Gabilondo denounced on January 7th, 2010 in the newscast that he presented on the Spanish TV channel 4 that belongs to CNN News in his daily column, how the pharmaceutical companies and the World Health Organization had sown the terror for economic reasons and concluded by saying that the most disgusting business was the business of fear.

On the other hand, now anyone who has any doubts about vaccines is expelled from public life, so it is not surprising that many think that what happened with influenza A in 2009 was a trial for what is happening now, especially since the mainstream media since the Covid-19 pandemic have stopped questioning the Big Phama's lack of ethics and questioning everything that comes out of the World Health Organization, which would be the normal task to do in order to fulfill the social function of critical journalism.

However, we have, for example, the British magazine The Economist, which serves as one of the official spokesmen for ideas and the globalist agenda, that has dedicated furious attacks on all those who have reservations against the new vaccines, calling them skeptical and deniers. In this way there is an article in The Economist with an illustration in which two people appear who do not want to get vaccinated and who are hiding, which is a way of demonizing anyone who considers that maybe vaccines for Covid -19 are not as good as they are telling us.

In this way in this article of The Economist the writer says in almost at the last paragraph: "It is likely that marginal opinions will spread when people lose confidence in their leaders. Therefore, the most effective vaccine against the nonsense launched by anti-vaccines is that the Government simply in its vaccination programs against Covid apply it as quickly as possible to avoid problems and errors."

And it also adds The Economist "When the elites do their job well, the populists and the crackpots have nothing to say."

This unique way of thinking reminds us of what was the lifelong tactic in the former Soviet Union, in which many of the dissidents were put in asylums because the rulers did not want to understand that someone was a dissident in the homeland of socialism.

By the way, there was a year in the 1980s that the director of the psychiatric hospitals for dissidents in the Soviet Union was awarded a Nobel Prize, just as the former USA

Secretary of the State, Henry Kissinger, was awarded the Nobel Peace Prize in 1973, who has even been accused of violation of Human Rights.

Thus in the above-mentioned quote from The Economist magazine about people who doubt about the administration of Covid-19 vaccines, they not only say that the rest of the people, that is, those of us who do not follow their line of thought are populists and nuts, but that the Economist magazine considers itself as a defender of the elites and says it openly. In this way in order to understand what they are trying to say we just have to know how to read a little between the lines.

In this way there are serious doubts about the administration of Covid-19 vaccines in the population because basically when we talk to doctors they tell us that the process of preparing the vaccines has been too fast, and even the pharmaceutical companies and the laboratories themselves in the public documents that are available to everyone on their web pages raise serious doubts about certain aspects of the Covid-19 vaccines, for example, that they are not able to guarantee that the vaccines do not sterilize, that it is said by the company Pfizer itself.

In addition to these doubts about the Covid-19 vaccines, on December 9, 2020, a series of documents were stolen or leaked from the European Medicines Agency. The official information says that they were stolen, although it is possible that these documents were leaked because there are always good people in all the places, from the archives of the European Medicines Agency and they were published on the internet, being only accessed through the Dark Web and therefore only through anonymous browsers like Thor. So these documents pertain primarily to the Pfizer vaccine evaluation process and there are variants of emails and reports that show how officials of the European Medicines Agency asked the European authorities to skip the national authorization processes.

These officials have said to justify themselves that they asked that all national authorization processes be skipped so that the vaccine could reach all countries at the same time, that is, that a reduction of national sovereignty was requested, which is typical of the globalist agenda. But in addition, the data revealed qualitative differences between the commercial batches and those used during clinical trials, that is, they were not the same vaccines. This is what has been published in some media platforms as a result of the report released by the French newspaper "Le Monde", an official media outlet par excellence.

But what nobody says when it comes to this question is that the efficacy of the Pfizer vaccine as reflected in these documents was only of 19%.

It is noteworthy that it was even suggested that the vaccine is more effective in people who only receive one dose than in people who have received both doses. But the truth is that in these documents the percentage of effectiveness that appears is only 19%, which has caused the European Medicines Agency to denounce the theft of the information and say that indeed that documentation has been stolen from them but that it has been manipulated by hackers..

Although it is impossible to know if this information was manipulated by hackers or not, what the European Medicines Agency could do to deny the efficacy of 19% of Pfizer vaccines is to publish the original document that shows the correct percentage of efficacy.

In a similar way, an alleged letter that Donald Trump wrote to Joe Biden and that in theory he left him in the White House office in which he said: "You know that I won (the election), Biden," could also be easily disproved if Biden published the original letter.

But it must also be taken into account that this information is above all conversations that the officials had with each other, emails, etc., that is, they are not the final reports. In fact, what these documents suggest is that there was a validation process with discussions, because indeed at the beginning the effectiveness of the Pfizer vaccine was not as expected, but that finally everyone agreed so that this efficacy was the desired one and validated it.

In fact, in one of the reports presented by the pharmaceutical company Pfizer to the Government of the United Kingdom, which was one of the first reports they presented, it is specified that the effectiveness is greater than 90% whilst the whole issue of the secondary effects is discussed. Pfizer recognizes that it is not able to guarantee that its vaccine against Covid-19 does not sterilize, basically because it has not tested it in pregnant women, and because it does not know if the administration of the vaccine today may cause sterility after a few years sight. All these doubts about the vaccine are normal since a vaccine usually takes between 5 to 10 years to be developped whilst some vaccines are not even developed because the magic formula is not reached

In fact, the president himself of the Junta de Extremadura, which is the government of the autonomous community of Extremadura in Spain, in a press conference at the beginning of 2021 said that the mass vaccination in nursing homes was being carried out first to see the evolution of the drug, which means that the elderly are being used as human guinea pigs. He also said that depending on how they saw how the vaccines were going, they would so do.

On the other hand, it is very curious that while in the end in Europe the commercialization and administration of the Pfizer vaccine to the population was approved, in the United States the arrival of this same vaccine was delayed despite the fact that Trump pressed for it to come out before US presidential election on November 3, 2020, whilst the US Food and Drug Administration (FDA) itself did not want to approve it so quickly.

Therefore, it is normal to have doubts regarding the Covid-19 vaccines, and rather it is reckless not to have them. In addition, there are deaths from direct or indirect causes derived from vaccination, whilst we still do not really know the effectiveness of the vaccine, being used especially the elderly population as guinea pigs.

In any case, it is quite obvious that the fact of being vaccinated or not should be voluntary, although it will not be voluntary either, since there will be a Covid passport which is part of the Great Reset plan and of the 2030 agenda.

Therefore, doubting about the vaccines is prudent and even recommended, without even discussing about the difference of messenger RNA vaccines, such as the Pfizer and Moderna ones, compared to traditional vaccines, which obviously would pose even more doubts to most people regarding the effectiveness and safety of the Covid-19 vaccines.

In this way if we say that simply the problem with the Covid-19 vaccines is that they are not effective enough and that they also generate a series of side effects that are not too serious, these ideas would already be enough to generate doubts and be prudent with the administration of these vaccines.

Although the obvious truth is that Covid-19 vaccines are being experimented on in humans since the official website of the United States government "ClinicalTrials.gov" says that the study and trial dates for the Pfizer vaccine are:

Actual study start date: April 29, 2020

Estimated Primary Completion Date: October 29, 2021

Estimated completion date of the study: April 6, 2023

And for the Moderna vaccine, the ClinicalTrials.gov website indicates that the studies and trial dates of the vaccine are:

Actual Study Start Date: July 27, 2020

Estimated Primary Completion Date: October 27, 2022

Estimated completion date of the study: October 27, 2022

Therefore, even the primary phase of study and trials of these vaccines are future dates at the time that I am writing this book, which I am doing in mid-April 2021, that is, with the vaccines that are being administered from Pfizer and Moderna is being experimented on with humans, and therefore the same happens with the rest of the vaccines such as the AstraZeneca one for example.

But it is also that there is a direct relationship between mass vaccination and the globalist agenda, which is embodied in our days in the 2030 agenda promoted by the World Economic Forum through the Great Reset, since for example there is a campaign launched by the Spanish Government which is called "solidarity vaccination". In this way, the logo of the 2030 agenda also appears in the logo of this solidarity vaccination campaign, which is obviously not by chance.

But what does the 2030 agenda have to do with mass vaccination?

In fact, at first, the 2030 Agenda did not propose any kind of role for pharmacology in the 2030 agenda, but rather, the multinational pharmaceutical companies had to be well controlled legislatively. But now the 2030 agenda has changed and the big technology multinationals (Big Tech), the big pharmaceutical multinationals (Big Pharma) and the big banks (Big Bank) may work as they wish, but It is the rest of the people who are not able to work as they wish, since we have restrictions on mobility and on the opening of businesses and censorship.

So these pharmaceutical companies have permanent state funding, since for example these Spanish companies have a great global vaccination campaign behind that must be defended, whose main objective is to help guarantee fair, affordable and universal access to the vaccine as a "global public good".

In this way, with the excuse of fair, affordable and universal access to vaccines as a public good, they are experimenting with the vaccines in humans, especially now with the elderly.

On this, for example, the Spanish Government is based, which has sold Covid-19 vaccines to its nearby Principality of Andorra while health professionals in Spain could not use them, whilst false debates are opened about whether a mayor has received the vaccine or not, which are just ways to distract and divert attention from the real problems that have to do with the vaccines. It has even been said that there are people who are taking advantage of being in power to get vaccinated, when the truth is that there are many people who do not want to get the vaccine against Covid-19 because they have doubts about it, just like the politicians themselves have them.

In this way, the same Spanish Government as President Maduro of Venezuela have said in an unsubtle way, is going to wait for all those who need to be vaccinated to do it first, which obviously implies that they want others to be experimented with vaccinations before the Government gets the vaccine.

In fact, we should all be able to decide for ourselves whether or not to get the Covid-19 vaccine by doing a risk-benefit analysis, but as the globalist agenda says that the objective of "solidarity" vaccination is to help guarantee fair, affordable and universal access to the vaccine as a global public good, then they are really telling us that vaccination is going to be so recommended that if we do not agree to get vaccinated we will be anti-vaccine deniers, and therefore it will be fair if we cannot enter the stores, travel or do anything because of it.

So, according to the globalist agenda, if 0.5%, 1%, 2% of the world population is going to die from vaccines, it does not matter, because the globalist magnates see us as cattle and not as people, and in fact for decades they have looking for ways to reduce the world population.

In this way, the globalist oligarchies eliminate the essence of the human being, his freedom, his responsibility, all his values, etc. And now we depend on governments to do what the World Health Organization tells them to do, which is an organization funded and controlled by the Bill and Melinda Gates Foundation and other globalist moguls, which requires vaccination not to be voluntary, but rather a list is made of those who are not vaccinated, a list that will be shared with other countries, as the former Spanish Minister of Health Salvador Illa said on the Spanish television channel "La Sexta."

Thus Salvador Illa literally said in the program "Al Rojo vivo" (Red Hot): "we will create a registry and share it with our European partners of those residents in Spain who have been offered the vaccine and have simply rejected it."

It is obvious that his list of those who have not wanted to be vaccinated would go against the Data Protection Law, but in fact the data protection laws are among the laws most violated by many governments of many nations.

In fact, the Prime Minister of the United Kingdom himself, Boris Johnson, said that he was not going to make a list of people who did not want to be vaccinated, and immediately the Minister of Health of the United Kingdom came out saying not to pay attention to what the Prime Minister had just said .

For these reasons it is obvious that many governments of nations are going to make a list of people who do not want to get the Covid-19 vaccine, and this is where the concept of the Covid passport comes in, which in theory in mid-2021 according to the agenda of this project, should have been implemented globally.

In fact, Denmark already announced on January 13, 2021 that those who had received the vaccine could circumvent mobility restrictions for the time being and in the near future they could possibly circumvent others.

Of course, regarding Covid passports, the articles can be found on the World Economic Forum website that celebrate the arrival of these Covid passports, since all those who participate in the Davos Forum are social engineers with a desire to control people. So whenever we enter the website of the World Economic Forum we can read between the lines the idea that they are the ruling elite and that the rest of the people are fools who do not know what is best for them; therefore they tell us that we should not be eating meat but grass and worms, that we have to give up heating ourselves with certain energy sources and that we need now a Covid passport that tells others whether we are vaccinated or not in order to be able to buy, travel, etc.

In this way, Microsoft has been developing the technology for many months to create digital documents that show the vaccination status of every individual. In fact, the Covid passport project is the first step of the global digital identification project, ID2020.

This coalition of companies, among which we find Microsoft and many other technological companies that work in conjunction with a Foundation called Commons Project, around which the Covidian (related to Covid) passport is articulated, which is chaired by Mr. Brad Perkins, who has worked in the RAND corporation, a military intelligence corporation, that is to say, pure American deep state, and has also worked in the company "Human Longevity" that are dedicated to genetic experiments to achieve human longevity. Brad Perkins is in charge of the Covid passport project and is also a collaborator of the Atlanta epidemic center, which is known worldwide as the

CDC (Center for Disease Control and Prevention) which is a world reference in the fight against epidemics and shows us the path that awaits us.

In this way Brad Perkins has given several interviews lately presenting the Covid passport project in which he said: "For a while most of us will have to show and prove that we have had a negative COVID-19 test, or that we are in a state of updated vaccination to carry out the normal routines of our lives". So we are not going to get the vaccine only once, but we are going to be vaccinated several times for several years at least, which obviously is an ocean of profitability for pharmaceutical companies, considering that they will have to develop new vaccines if the virus strain varies, which it is going to obviously do.

And as for having an updated vaccination status to carry out the normal routines of our lives, it does not mean only to be able to travel, since Brad Perkins adds that we must have an updated vaccination status "either by getting on a plane and going to another country, whether to go to work, school, the supermarket or any type of event. "

Thus, we can remember that in the case of air travel, for example, there are countries where passengers arrived and there was a man with a digital pistol thermometer, who pointed it at the forehead of the passengers, then he or she would verify that they did not have a fever, the passengers would be asked if they had been to China in the last 15 days, etc. and these passengers would enter the country of destination without further ado. That is why the figure of the asymptomatic people is so key in this issue because if there is someone who is a carrier of the virus and does not have symptoms, these types of preventive mechanisms such as measuring our temperature with a thermometer no longer make sense, which also means that it eliminates all preventive activity because we can all be carriers of the virus and spread it, which is at least what the official version proposes.

In this way what science has done so far is to investigate, so whenever something new comes out it is investigated and many ideas are shared, hypotheses are made, then the hypotheses confirm each other, and finally the hypotheses have to be demonstrated with experiments, which is known as the scientific method. Thus in the scientific method, professionals raise doubts and hypotheses and in this way participate in the process of seeking the truth, but now this questioning of hypotheses and reality is censored.

Continuing with the issue of the vaccination passport in which they are working, this passport is based on the technology baptized as "the Common Pass", whose development is carried out by this Foundation together with the World Economic Forum, who have a company together called Common Trust which is publicized on the website of the World Economic Forum.

The key to all this is that in order to carry out our daily activities they want us to trust Big Pharma, governments and the World Health Organization by giving us a vaccine that even the laboratories themselves say can sterilize and cause another series of secondary effects. This is what the program led by Microsoft is based on, which is not something hidden, but has also been published by an official media outlet such as the New York Times, of which there are also videos on YouTube which have been censored by the way.

So we may ask ourselves the following, how can it be that doctors do not even know the degree of efficiency or effectiveness of vaccines? What we know about it is due to the leaks of the documents of the European Medicines Agency, due to the evident increase in infections and secondary effects that these same vaccines are causing, but we really do not know the real efficiency or effectiveness of these vaccines.

All this type of information about the adverse effects of Covid-19 vaccines appears in some media and not in others, and so in the case of Israel, as most of the people in this country have already been vaccinated, they are using their population to experiment in humans with these vaccines.

So, how can it be that the efficacy and efficiency of vaccines or their adverse effects in the medium and long term are still not well known, and despite everything the Covid passport, which is an electronic passport, has already been designed and is even beginning to be implemented to certify people's vaccination status?. In other words, the Covid passport has been designed before the vaccines themselves.

Precisely the UN project ID2020 also financed by Bill Gates' Microsoft is about to mark us all digitally as cows, a project in which the Gavi Foundation is involved, which is the alliance for the global vaccination of Bill Gates as well.

According to Gavi's own website, its impact is based on the strengths of its main partners, the World Health Organization, UNICEF, the World Bank and the Bill and Melinda Gates Foundation. In addition, Gavi also works with donors, including sovereign governments, private sector foundations, and corporate partners; NGOs, advocacy groups, professional and community associations, religious organizations, and academia; vaccine manufacturers, including those in emerging markets; research institutes and technical health; and governments of the implementing countries.

Now Gavi has appointed its founder, Dakota Gruener, as executive director of the ID2020 project, and whose president of Gavi is José Manuel Durao Barroso, former president of Portugal between 2002 and 2004 and former president of the European Commission between 2004 to 2014. In addition, as always, the Rockefeller Foundation supports Gavi as it usually does with other globalist projects.

Moreover none of this is really hidden, so it is neither theory nor conspiracy, since if we go to the Gavi, ID2020 websites, etc. we can find the founding partners with all these names.

So there are two problems, the first is that when we go to the website of one of these globalist entities like the Rockefeller Foundation, we immediately realize that they are talking to us about the 2030 globalist agenda with some variation in some sentence, and the second problem is that the David Rockefeller himself confessed in a memoir published in 2001 that there was a globalist project and that there was a secret cabal to which he and his family belonged, and that they were looking for a global world and that also if that was the accusation he would plead guilty and he was proud to be.

So the fact that these globalist movements exist is quite normal, that is, there are people with money and power that desire to control the world a bit, but for that it is assumed that there is a political system from which these people, if they are voted, could lead society, but now even this system seems to be over and everything seems to be hijacked.

So right now the Common Project has many civil servants, company representatives, etc. who are already designing a platform which they are prepared to implement, whose objective, according to the documents that are already being analyzed and are being viewed, will be that this platform decides above the governments and regardless of what the citizens want, if the data provided by the individuals regarding their vaccination or health status, allow them to obtain the pass to carry out activities of daily life, even to buy food. This has even been said by the president of the RAND corporation, Brad Perkins, who has also worked for years at the CDC (Center for Disease Control and Prevention of Atlanta, United States) and who is also in charge of the Common Project.

So we may wonder if at work it is going to be possible to dismiss (lay off) workers if they do not get vaccinated, and the answer is that it will be possible to dismiss them since even the European unions have positioned themselves in this way in this regard.

By the way, the head of the world union organization is also in the photo of the Council for Inclusive Capitalism along with Pope Francis as one of "our guardians" as they are called. So many of the same actors who are in several of these supranational global entities that want to impose the globalist agenda appear again and again on other globalist projects.

In this way, already in the manifesto of the ID2020 project, that identification project by which they want us all to be digitally identified and created long before the arrival of the Covid, it was already stated in point number 8 that "this new model of digital identity global will not have a spontaneous acceptance by the population, so it would be necessary to change the perception of public opinion about this global census system by electronic means. "

In other words, this global digital identity system will not be popular, nor will people want it, but the popular will does not matter to these globalist tycoons and therefore they already confess that they will take care of that and in the end people will want or at least consent to the implications of the ID2020 project.

So it seems that these globalist oligarchies have doubts about how to implement global identity and then the Covid-19 arrived, so many agendas were put aside because they saw that this was an opportunity, as the president of the World Economic Forum says that it could not be missed out to accelerate the implementation of the globalist agenda, although quite possibly the most exact reality is that Covid-19 was created to accelerate the implementation of this agenda. In other words, the plandemic (planned pandemic) was created in order to impose the globalist agenda and not the other way around, that is that the Covid-19 arrived just coincidentally at the precise moment that the globalist elites needed it.

Thus, the president of the World Economic Forum, Klaus Schwab, says that this opportunity offered by the arrival of the Covid-19 cannot be missed and that it must be used to create a new society, a new social contract based on the fourth industrial revolution, on transhumanism, on total control and planetary socialism. This is not a conspiracy theory, but it is a globalist conspiracy.

In fact, it is a conspiracy that is progressively mutating, so regarding the fact that the Covid passport it will be a QR code that when scanned will indicate whether we are vaccinated or not, politicians have known it for a long time that it was already prepared because some politicians have already talked about a QR code ahead of time, and they know that previously they were considering implementing a system in which people had different colors (green, yellow, red, blue, etc.) depending on whether we were vaccinated or not and according to other health characteristics, which can be easily checked on the internet.

Thus, the companies in charge of applying this program in Spain are Indra, which is a technological defense company (Spanish deep state), the French computer consulting company Capgemini, to which the Spanish Government has offered the service without any advertising, without any public auction or no other process for awarding the service of managing the Covid-19 vaccination data, that is, it will be effectively responsible for the vaccination registry in Spain.

And with respect to the data itself of the vaccination registry, the multinational Accenture will be commissioned in Spain to do it, which "by chance" is also one of the sponsors of the ID2020 project together with the Rockefeller Foundation and Bill Gates.

In addition, in Spain, the SAS group has been awarded the design of the services for the exploitation of information on diagnostic tests of COVID-19, including the geolocation of people. And who's who within the SAS technological group? The executive director of the SAS Institute incorporated is James Goodnight since 1976, a billionaire and director of the World Economic Forum.

So as we see all these contracts go to companies and people who are part of the globalist agenda, and in fact there are many more companies involved, connections that exist and that can be found on the internet if someone has the time and knows how to find them. In fact, more and more freelancers are dedicated to finding these companies and connections because most journalists have stopped reporting on it.

9

Censorship in the 21st century. The fact-checking industry

As published by various media and Microsoft itself on its official website, Microsoft has created an alliance between technological companies and the media that will reinforce the censorship of Big Tech (large technology multinationals). Bill Gates has created a new alliance between companies, media and technology multinationals to "fight against disinformation on the Internet." This new Ministry of World Truth is promoted by Microsoft, the billionaire's company, and aims to go beyond the censorship that the Big Tech is imposing on independent media and voices. This Alliance has a committee led by Microsoft who will work worldwide and it seems that few will be able to escape the scrutiny and surveillance of the Coalition for the Provenance and Authenticity of Content (C2PA), as it is called.

Based on the agreement that Microsoft published on February 22, 2021, some of the founders of this great coalition of "certifiers of truthfulness" comprise it for now The New York Times, the BBC news corporation, multinationals such as Adobe, the software company ARM, Intel and the makers of Truepic, an application that allows you to verify images to ensure that no one has tampered with them. Microsoft has loaded on words his project with good intentions (saying that they have good intentions) and ensures that it is only about preserving "the integrity of the content", and that the verifiers will be able to verify that "the original information has not been manipulated along the way".

However, by thoroughly reading the documents related to the Coalition for Provenance and Authenticity of Content, the Microsoft surveillance committee would also reinforce the international network of Fact-Checking agencies or "content verifiers", all of them left-wing and financed mostly by the so-called GAFTA (Google, Amazon, Facebook, Apple and Twitter). In this sense, Microsoft will implement algorithms and software that allow identifying what type of content, whether text, image, video or document, was created by a generalist media outlet such as The New York Times or by an alternative digital media outlet or just created by a user. So in the event that the news comes from a media outlet or source that challenges and questions the information published by The New York Times, it will immediately be classified as Fake News. Another novelty of Bill Gates' C2PA alliance is to trace the trajectory of the "fake" content even when released by an anonymous user. In this way, Bill Gates will offer to the Big Tech companies software that will allow them to track information that their Coalition believes is "misleading", be it an article on a blog, a video on a platform, a paragraph on a social network or a meme. In any case, both the author and those who have consumed this false news will be identified. On this, Microsoft states that the investigation will pursue "from the capture device to the information consumer." For this reason, "Collaboration with chip makers, news organizations, software and platform companies is critical to facilitating a comprehensive provenance standard and driving broad adoption across the ecosystem content." says the Microsoft representative. The great Coalition will have the support of Project Origin, which is another of Microsoft's organizations that is already designing standards and technologies that certify the source and provenance of online content. "This is an important step forward to address the growing concerns with the manipulation and fabrication of news and information," which can be read on its website.

In this way, Bill Gates seems to have formed a sinister alliance or confederation, as the New York Times itself has a terrifying record of errors, misinformation, falsehoods, plagiarism, etc. in their news, now turning out to be the measuring stick of journalistic information.

In this way, this alliance will use a technological solution that determines the origin of the information and its veracity in order to combat misleading content, which is another way to avoid saying that it is an alliance to eliminate content that does not follow the official version of the single thought, which is the most important objective and differential element for the constitution of this alliance. In addition, with this technology, it will be possible to know which people have read certain information, thus finishing with the laws of protection of personal data, being possible to reach the homes or even the mobile devices of users who read any alternative media news.

In fact, they may already have started to do so. But the terrible thing about the matter is that the pattern of the Spanish Inquisition is repeated since the fault lies not only with the author, the printer or the program through which this information is channeled, but also with whoever accesses the information. That is just as it was forbidden to read certain books centuries ago and not just to write them, print them or go to see them, the same thing happens now. In other words, they are going to persecute the one who channels this information, the one from whom the information originated and the poor unfortunates who have read, seen or heard it.

Thus, one of the protagonists of this alliance is Eric Horvitz, who is the scientific director of Microsoft, since they, as social engineers, devise and propose these globalist projects, although later there are others who execute them. In this way although Eric Horvitz has been the one who has announced this project and is the scientific director of Microsoft, Bill Gates obviously continues to direct the designs of the company in the shadow. But when we happen to read a little about the promotion that Eric Horvitz has done on Microsoft's own website of this project, he makes the statement about the alliance that we have just mentioned, appearing also on the website an article by him defending the idea about this project a little bit, which in a curious way begins his text explaining that all this has occurred to him at the World Economic Forum, which is not surprising knowing the type of people who meet at the Davos Forum.

As we have already explained, the World Economic Forum is the promoter of the idea of the Great Reset, and thus Erick Horvitz in an article that also is accompanied by a video in which he appears on a television set, suggests that its objective is to develop and deploy technologies to certify the origin and the authenticity of the information. He says that what must be done is a kind of traceability such as that carried out, for example, with food products to guarantee where they come from and to know, for example, where a certain product has been grown, which would prove that this product has a certain quality. But in the case of information it does not matter where it comes from, since the truth is the truth, regardless of the media outlet or the person who says it.

In this way, regarding news and information it is not relevant who has said or written it but whether it is true or not, therefore this Alliance also wants to determine what is true and what is not. Moreover Erick Horvitz also raised that he had been told at the 2019 World Economic Forum that this project should be done, being the fact that the Project Origin already existed at that time and it is the umbrella on which this initiative depends.

In this way it seems that they use many companies in a similar manner as when money is offered looking to find a front company in order for the money to reach its destination, then current accounts are opened in order to make it impossible to keep track of the money as well. So it seems that this is what they do, those who allegedly are the defenders of traceability, since they hide in a sea of acronyms, in a sea of projects that are created by the same globalist companies and oligarchies.

In this way the bigger the number of companies, alliance names, acronyms, etc. the more it provides a greater sense of universality, making feel that this project has immense social support, making it more difficult to determine responsibilities or guilty ones about it. In this way, faced with a bunch of companies, acronyms and alliances, we get distracted and even fail to think that those of the Alliance for the verification of the contents and the Project Origin are the same ones that are also in the Bilderberg Club, in the Trilateral Commission, in the Foundations of George Soros, in the Council for Inclusive Capitalism, in the World Economic Forum, etc.

This is how it is about the new oligarchies that continue to have the old ambition, the old corruption, the old inquisition, but all disguised as novelty with new names.

In addition to the New York Times, another of the founders of this coalition of "truth certifiers" is the British network BBC, which is another of the reference media, which has a very good reputation since journalists and other professionals have spent years saying that public televisions should be like the BBC, even when the BBC scandals were piling up. In other words, the BCC corporation achieved a good reputation that has been maintained for years despite the scandals.

In addition, Eric Horvitz and Microsoft say that they have created a platform to give shape precisely to this technological solution that Microsoft has announced, being in a position to implement It, although perhaps they may have already started to implement it without us knowing. In this way, Eric Horvitz said that the objective is to create a pipeline in which the origin of the information goes to its receiver, having this pipeline shielded and being Microsoft the one that shields it. That is, there is no type of external vigilant or auditor that will verify the information except for Microsoft, and even if someone tells the same facts but gives it another interpretation or another nuance, it will be qualified and crossed out as fake news

And another of the elements is also the Initiative for the Authenticity of the Content, which is basically the same idea but in which we also find Twitter and the newspaper USA Today. In the end, it is a salad of acronyms of all kinds that in recent years has been configured as a spider web led by Microsoft in this case, whilst Google is leading another initiative.

Thus, the objectives of this project are mainly two, which is what the Microsoft statement says, being the first to control the information, determining what is disinformation when the members of this alliance consider it appropriate and the second, to locate both the origin of each information and the receiver. So at least in this case Microsoft is being transparent with its intentions or rather blatant because sometimes It is not only necessary to have power, but also to say who and in what way has the power.

But what Microsoft does not say is that it is using many resources in a program to promote a digital census under the umbrella of the ID2020 project, which we have already spoken about on more than one occasion and which is related to this new alliance. In this way the company that Bill Gates founded is working with its large staff of programmers to create a directory of people that, according to the company itself, will allow to have a decentralized, private and general-use digital identity, that is, it will be a system that allows or denies access to our most precious private information, in addition to being able to adequately track when a company or application checks these data out, as long as it is not Microsoft who does it.

But the problem is: who is watching the watchdog, which in this case is Microsoft?

But as much as they insist on telling us that it is a decentralized database, this directory is not, since it is centralized by its creator. Instead, the technology that is decentralized is, for example, Bitcoin and the entire blockchain structure or the entire blockchain infrastructure platform but not the Microsoft database. Although there is today on the internet data saying that Bitcoin has already been intervened by the big investment funds.

In addition, this project is part of another initiative, that is, it is one of the initiatives of the "Identity Foundation" that is also being promoted by the World Economic Forum, which thanks to the pandemic manipulates the public opinion so that people won't consider this type of world census or database a threat. In fact, this is the work of the World Economic Forum as well, that is, to make propaganda about it so that this world database is taken into account, and thus they advertise it as something positive on their website. In this way, there is an article defending this initiative on the World Economic Forum website, in which there is a photo that they use to illustrate the text with three children of different races and cultures, because obviously the project must be inclusive, which in fact means globalist and supremacist.

This is how they advocate for this digital identity so that no child goes hungry, which is the argument that is being used, but the reality is that they implement censorship, which does not help children stop starving. In this way this census that they intend to do is which everything else is based on, because the traceability of information from the origin to the receiver cannot be implemented if the digital identity of both people is not known or tracked. So for this reason everyone has to be within that digital system controlled by Microsoft, that is, it would be a database of all the citizens of the planet.

So what is the problem with this world database? The problem is where so much data is stored, being at this point where Microsoft's initiative to use synthetic DNA comes in.

Regarding genetic DNA, the World Economic Forum has also been talking a lot about it, since its president Klaus Schwap is a recognized transhumanist. In this way Microsoft is already buying several million strands of synthetic DNA from the company Twist Bioscience. So how do people get synthetic DNA?. If we enter the website of one of these companies, specifically Twist Bioscience, we can upload the DNA sequence that we want which we previously download ourselves from the internet and in a couple of weeks later the personalized synthetic DNA is received in the mailbox at home by nine cents for each base pair, which is very cheap.

Over a decade ago the machines that made synthetic DNA were very expensive but now they are not, whilst the advocates of this technology are the architects of the Great Reset at the head, who also say that through this it will be possible to build a permanent source of useful compounds in drugs, which is what the World Economic Forum is involved more now, obviously on the issue of Covid, together with food production, which is also linked to the production and consumption of synthetic meat food, which is also being promoted by the World Economic Forum. In fact, Bill Gates has said that all first world countries should be producing and eating artificial meat.

In fact, Bill Gates himself in February 2021 appeared in a video drinking a glass of water that came from feces, which is an initiative that aims actually to solve the problem of sewage channeling in underdeveloped countries, creating toilets which themselves can somehow dehydrate the fecal waste and transform it into drinking water.

Continuing with the subject that concerns us with synthetic DNA, it is used to design materials never seen before, according to Microsoft. So it seems that they are talking once again about playing at being gods, of believing ourselves to be God directly, creating DNA on demand. In fact, as this can pose a risk to the national security of the United States and that of other countries, there are already specific national security units in the United States and in some other countries to find out to what extent this poses a threat to the national security of these countries, in the event that, for example, this type of technology is used to reconstruct, for example, the extinct smallpox virus.

So for example, from public access information in a few months and for less than one hundred thousand dollars, someone could mount a pandemic.

In fact, Gates himself, in one of his videos posted at the beginning of March 2021, raised the possibility of pandemics in the future released by laboratories, which is already perverse in fact. In this way we can understand that a laboratory may work to face a pandemic, but we would only be able to understand that a laboratory created a pandemic unless it has the worst intentions for mankind. Furthermore, the worst thing of all is that this is said by a man who has made many investments in laboratories and who in theory knows his colleagues well in the pharmaceutical sector. So even if we think that Microsoft's interests are good, there is anyways an obvious risk of laboratories creating pandemics.

What if the system is attacked or hacked?. Precisely Microsoft at the beginning of March 2021 denounced that hackers supported by the Government of China had taken advantage of the weaknesses of Microsoft's servers to gain access to information from several organizations in the United States on research on infectious diseases. The hackers also had access to information from companies such as law firms, universities, defense contractors, analytical centers, and non-governmental organizations. So the question that we should be asking ourselves would be: is Microsoft the multinational that is going to do the global digital census or the one that is going to specify the traceability of the information when they cannot even guarantee the security of their own servers? In fact, Microsoft is also the one behind the Covid passport and Common Pass technology, as we have seen in another chapter of this book.

So now it is not only about a health issue, but also about a cyber pandemic, because through cyberattacks digital pandemics can be created in the world.

Returning to the issue of censorship and disinformation, it is necessary to also talk about other elements like the news verifiers, the so-called fact-checking agencies, which are almost always from the political left, and not precisely from the moderate left, and who are dedicated to "verifying" the news.

In fact, the news-checker industry is relatively recent and was really boosted by the 2016 US presidential election, with a goal that was not hidden and was in fact publicized, which was to prevent it from happening again that a candidate not elected by the system or by the establishment could reach the White House, as happened with Donald Trump. That is when voices denouncing disinformation arose and paradoxically those voices were born from the traditional media that have been disinforming for decades. Thus, the growth of the news verifier industry arises precisely from the discrediting of traditional journalism, that in theory should be in charge of providing data and arguments so that citizens could get closer to the truth. Because if we know the truth as Jesus said in the bible, it will set us free.

But since most traditional media, instead of getting closer to the truth, long ago became pawns of the globalist agenda, then they have ceased to fulfill this social function and that is why these information verification companies arise, which from a point of view of spontaneous free market order would be fine. In other words, if the media cease to fulfill its function, then other agencies have to emerge.

Unfortunately, these data verification agencies have an important political component and are grouped around a network that is called International Fact-Checking Network (IFCN), that proclaims independence as one of their main values, although in reality they are financed by the large technological companies. Among these agencies in Spain we find the State agency "Efe", dependent on the government of the day, which is specifically called Efe Verifica (Efe Verifies), Newtral, which is anything but neutral, which obviously belongs to the slightly moderate political left, and which has reached an alliance with CEU, which is a university of the Catholic Church, which reminds us of the Spanish Inquisition of the Catholic Church that in the Middle Ages censored ideas or content that would question the vision of the church. In fact, CEU San Pablo University and Newtral.es have launched a master's degree in digital verification, fact-checking and data journalism, so this Catholic university seems to forget what Jesus said, that we will know the truth and the truth will make us free.

But why does a Catholic University like the CEU would want freedom when for centuries the Catholic Church has censored scientists and people of other religions for thinking differently?. In fact in the past the Catholic Church in one way or another have had centuries of experience pursuing freedom. In this way, the experience of centuries in repression and destruction of the freedom of the Catholic Church is combined with the new desire to destroy and repress the freedom of the promoters of the globalist agenda, such as those who meet in the Davos Forum.

Thus, in the case of the Spanish news verification company, fact-checking, it is Ana Pastor who is behind Newtral, which is the founder and sole partner. So it is nonsense for a global network of news verifiers to be created when there is a woman who is the founder and sole partner of one of the leading fact-checking companies in the country, who happens to be the wife of the also journalist of the Spanish television channel "La

Sexta", García Ferreras, who is one of those journalists who actively participated in the disinformation campaign after the Madrid train terrorist attacks on March 11, 2004.

And then we have a third leg which is called Maldita.es along with Efe Verifica and Newtral, which is directed by a journalist who also worked for the journalist García Ferreras and Ana Pastor. In fact, it is considered a daughter company of the journalists García Ferreras and Ana Pastor.

Precisely these news verification companies are the ones that use WhatsApp, Facebook, other social media platforms and Big Tech Apps to review and evaluate the accuracy of the content precisely on these platforms, limiting what they call "the harmful dissemination of false information". But what do they understand by false information? For the fact-checking agencies, the persecution of false information is one of their obvious lies, since anyone who questions the unique collectivist thinking of this new corporate socialism, and now with the pandemic, anyone who questions the official version of the Covid-19 crisis is persecuted and censored. In short, everything that clashes with the globalist agenda is what must be avoided from being said, read, heard, seen and even announced, even if the president of the United States does or says it, it must be also avoided and censored.

Thus the New York Post, which is a lifelong official newspaper along with the New York Times and one of the deans of the North American press, published the entire corruption scandal of the Biden family of the president of the United States, and then everything about is censored and disappears from the social media platforms. Even in the collective madness that was created in the weeks leading up to the US presidential elections of November the 3rd 2020, Twitter went so far as to censor the United States House of Representatives itself, that is to say it is no longer that they censor the top politician in the United States, but rather a collective political chamber such as the United States House of Representatives, which would be like putting a muzzle on all the representatives, whilst unfairly blaming Russia for example of having hacked and erased the comments of the House of Representatives.

In addition, the lack of independence of these news verification agencies is so evident that on the few occasions in which these agencies have established criteria that have gone against the interests of Google, Facebook, Microsoft and other technological companies, they have been called publicly to order.

Moreover then the United Nations makes rankings of countries according to freedom of the press, etc. but it is even worse because the above-mentioned International Fact-

Checking Network belongs to an organization called the Poynter Institute, an organization that is theoretically philanthropic and non-profit based in Florida. Precisely we have to be alert when an organization declares itself non-profit, because then we have to ask ourselves what exactly they gain from the activities they do.

Although the truth is that in the United States there are many entities that are non-profit organizations because that allows not to pay taxes, while in Spain, for example, being a non-profit entity can help to get government subsidies but not to be exempt of paying taxes, which is in fact what many entities linked to parties or unions or Catholic religious orders do in Spain. But in the case of the United States, in many cases what is sought is the legal title of an organization of this type because it is exempt from taxes.

Related to or under the Poynter Institute are other agencies, other institutions, and other foundations. So when we go to check who are those who finance the Poynter Institute we begin to discover a large number of our usual suspects who always appear behind globalist social engineering projects. In this case, a new entity appears which is the Knight Foundation, which is closely associated with the CIA, which many independent researchers attribute to being part of the North American deep State. But then the usual suspects appear as funders of the Poynter Institute, that is, the Bill and Melinda Gates Foundation, Google itself, the MacArthur Foundation and George Soros' Open Society. And in addition, the Omidyar Network organization also injects funds into the Poynter Institute, which is owned by the businessman Pierre Omidyar, founder of eBay and known for helping the Democratic Party of the United States to seek Russian interference in everything that affects the globalist agenda. He is also a regular contributor to George Soros' projects and was involved in the political process in Ukraine. In fact it is known by many journalists that George Soros also financed the Euromaidan Ukrainian Revolution from November 30, 2013 to February 2014, being in turn Pierre Omidyar also a regular contributor or collaborator to George Soros and also involved in the political process in Ukraine.

By the way, there is a very good investigation from "Russia Today" that shows that the United States Agency for International Development, USAID, for its acronym in English, in which there are many usual suspects of the globalist agenda, along with the American embassy in Kiev and Pierre Omidyar launched a television channel to participate in the propaganda of the Euromaidan Revolution, which ended with the overthrow of pro-Russian President Viktor Yanukovych. But Pierre Omidyar is also very well related to Hillary Clinton, with Obama, with the military industrial complex of the

United States and among other activities he has sponsored and owns The Intercept, which is a publication who has released documents stolen by Edward Snowden, that is a former US computer intelligence consultant who copied and leaked highly classified information from the National Security Agency (NSA) in 2013 when he was an employee and subcontractor of the Central Intelligence Agency (CIA), although some people doubt that he has ever stopped being a spy at some point, since he himself said that he did not trust the New York Times because it withheld information and then decided that it was better to go to the newspaper "The Guardian".

And in 2018 the aforementioned Ebay founder launched a group called The Luminate Group, and of course if we go to their website they tell us that they have very good intentions but in reality they are part of the globalist agenda with spurious interests. In fact, the Luminate group finances journalistic projects around the world and an extensive network of NGOs also, in addition to receiving grants from Soros and Pierre Omidyar. For its part, the Poynter Institute collaborates actively with the United States government and has been contracted by the United States Agency for Global Media and the State Department to finance educational projects on information verification, of which some projects are in Latin America, and in concrete one of them in Bolivia.

By the way one of the entities that also fights against "fake news" in the United States and that works with Facebook is the Politifact platform, which also belongs to the Poynter Institute and is also financed by the Ford Foundation.

So as we may see these organizations or people are the same ones as always, committing the very same misdeeds, claiming the power to decide what is true and what is false to the point of locating even the people who have accessed the information that will be eliminated. It is also necessary to remember the collaboration of the Poynter Institute with The Weekly Standard, one of the publications that defended most strongly that there were weapons of mass destruction in Iraq, and that the president cooperated with the terrorist organization Al Qaeda, because once It was discovered that there are no weapons of mass destruction in Iraq the only way to mess with this nation was by saying that it cooperated with Al Qaeda.

In this way if we enter the website of the World Economic Forum and in the search engine that is on this website we write "Poynter" many results and references appear, because the Poynter Institute collaborates in making the corporatist social propaganda of the World Economic Forum. In fact, there is an article on the World Economic Forum website in which the Poynter group is quoted with the title "Hoax hunters: the team that tries to win the war on fake news", and when one investigates a little more realizes that the Poynter Institute is very versatile and in addition to working in the data verification industry, it also happens that it does studies on inequality, on climate change and also participates with pleasure in other campaigns such as the "Build back better " one, which means to rebuild better, slogan that has already been promoted by Joe Biden and that will appear a lot in the media outlets and social media platforms in the near future. In fact the "Build back better" is the economic project of the Democratic party that is currently in power in the United States with Joe Biden as president, which is included in the electoral program.

And another of the words that we are going to hear in schools is that of "media literacy", a concept that comes from UNESCO, a UN (United Nations) agency, which in theory are the ones that should protect children whilst in fact they intend to introduce a manipulated vision of reality into the classroom. It is a trap concept, because in theory what the UN should be pursuing is literacy in general, that is to say that everyone may have access to their own knowledge and criteria. In this way, in the age of the Internet, the economic barriers to accessing knowledge disappear, since almost anyone has access to practically free libraries of all kinds on the Internet.

However, we have reached a historical moment in which when we have all those possibilities to expand our knowledge through the internet and to have our own criteria, we have become functionally illiterate, and they want to teach children to learn to read the media communication with the criteria that globalist agents want, because the opposite of media literacy would be to have critical citizens with free thinking, backed by arguments, which is obviously that these oligarchies are not interested in. This why create agencies that determine what is true and what is not.

We are talking about supposed philanthropists with the financial power of non-profit foundations that work as true black money launderers and that allocate huge resources to the traditional media, and that once they are rejected by the public in the face of evidence that they are disinformation platforms at the service of the ruling power, then they themselves promote the creation of verification agencies to control social media, and ultimately to be able to control information throughout the web, from origin to receiver, that is the objective pursued by the coalition led by Microsoft.

However there is also a level of individual responsibility and we cannot put all the blame on the elites who have been promoting the destruction of education for years, but we have to be critical of what we read and the news that the traditional media tell us, since now when citizens lack criteria and are defenseless against misinformation, then the same ones who have created the problems offer the solution, that is, large technological companies ensure the traceability of messages along with the verification agencies to determine what it is true and what is not.

So we should care about investigating and scratching the surface even just a little, since in the world in which we live, globalist rulers and oligarchies tell us so many lies that with a little effort many truths can be discovered. In fact, there are people locked in their homes thinking that they are going to die tomorrow from Covid-19 because they have been brainwashed through the news of official media, social media platforms or through the internet, and they are prepared to believe any type of message, be it build back better, Great Reset, media literacy or any other.

At the very least, let us help our children to have criteria and get them out of the unique thought that these elites want to mark in schools and universities. Let us teach our children and others to think and make decisions for themselves to the extent that we can.

10

Smart cities. The slave cities of the future

The idea of "smart" cities make up one more element of the ecosystem of the globalist agenda and its different faces and brands, projects that hope to take advantage of the COVID to accelerate the arrival of a supposedly more "sustainable, inclusive and resilient " world.

The concept of smart cities is important for the social architects of the new normal, who try to promote and incorporate it into collective thinking, that is to say trying to spread it among the public opinion. Although they are called smart cities, they seem to be designed precisely for the opposite of what their name indicates, that is, to further idiot society and turn human beings no longer into animals, but into things that are even worse, and into slaves of technology companies that will govern and control their every move through 5G technology and the Internet of Things (IoT).

In this way, if we go to the official website of the World Economic Forum, it says that these are cities that use information and communication technologies, the set of sensors and other devices that make up the Internet of Things to improve not only its operation, that of cities, but also the services it offers to its citizens. In this way they want us to believe like is always the case that the World Economic Forum are very good and that they want our good as well.

So since 5G technology is necessary to be able to implement the Internet of Things, they create a public spending program to invest in 5G technology so that telecommunications companies do not have to spend the money.

Some think that with the 5G technology some kind of conspiracy is taking place in the shadow but the truth is that this whole project is being done in front of us.

In fact, smart cities, the Internet of Things and 5G technology are decisive for this technocracy. In the end, it is an element that is integrated into the ecosystem of the globalist agenda and its different faces and brands. This globalist agenda is that of the 2030 Agenda and the Great Reset that can be found on the Davos Forum website and which we also talked about in the first book I wrote about it.

Thus, these projects hope to take advantage of the arrival of the Covid-19 to accelerate the arrival of a supposedly more sustainable, more inclusive world in which hunger, diseases and the whole pack of good concepts that they always want to sell us as global warming disappear, discrimination on the grounds of gender, the dissidents themselves, etc. will disappear.

In his day the prophets of the digital transformation of these smart cities were already speaking about it, so it is not a new concept but now the elites put it as an example of what to aspire to or achieve in the coming years, in a process that as it is evident, the pandemic (or plandemic, that is a planned pandemic) is accelerating, that is, it is accelerating the adoption of new technologies.

The implementation of these technologies is taking place and will take place by governments and large technological corporations jointly, through the use of public money, that is, with public debt because in theory the governments do not have public money at this time of Covid-19 crisis and that is why they have to issue public debt. Just as the economic and financial crisis after the arrival of the Covid is so big whilst there is also a fiscal crisis in all countries, that is to say that the collection of taxes from the countries is not enough to cover the expenses of the States, which also it is happening in the countries of northern Europe, then the financing of the States is done through debt, without there being great protests on the part of the people, despite the fact that the most basic rights of the people are being violated.

Thus, the Covid operation is being a success to gradually end the natural resistance that people have to getting their rights restricted or taken away, such as freedom of movement, of circulation, of opinion, of expression, etc. Although there are countries where it has ended up causing a totally opposite reaction and people do not seem to be submitting to the dictatorship of the oligarchs and rulers of the day, on the contrary in parts of the world such as Spain the implantation of fear has accentuated the attitude of submission of a population that barely protests the restrictions on their fundamental rights that are applied to them.

Continuing with the theme of smart cities and according to the information that official propagandists give us, they are saying that the objective is to create an efficient ecosystem for the internet of things and the ability to make use of accumulated data, which is the most important thing. As they say verbatim on the website of the World Economic Forum, all these data serve the rulers to improve the quality of life of people through the optimization of public transport, the care and monitoring of environmental conditions (climate change again), improving the offer of public services for citizens and offering a more inclusive, responsive and transparent government, which are the same terms that globalist oligarchies always use.

As we already know, the president of the World Economic Forum, Klaus Schwab, has been obsessed with the fourth industrial revolution for years and with the total implementation of technology in the political management of cities as he himself says that Covid-19 is a perfect opportunity to accelerate this process, although it is not the only one who thinks this way since there are organizations such as the Brookings Institution or the McKinsey consultancy, which are two habitual suspects of the globalist agenda that have collaborated with the Davos Forum itself in promoting global corporate socialism, that is that big tech companies rule smart cities in a socialist state.

In this way, Klaus Schwab himself in his book published in June 2020 "Covid-19: the Great Reset" states textually "the need to face the pandemic with all available means eliminated some of the related regulatory and legislative impediments with the adoption of telemedicine. In the future it is certain that more medical care will be provided remotely, in turn, this will accelerate the trend to develop more portable and home diagnostics such as smart toilets capable of tracking health data and performing health analyzes. "

In this manner we can already imagine the implications of a social system based on the massive collection of data without even having to leave the house, which is one more way to keep ourselves confined at home without going out. That is, if they can have all our health and privacy data without us leaving home, they already have one more reason to tell us not to leave home and not only to avoid contagion by a virus.

This way, these technological companies will be able to collect all our data when we are at home, whilst at the same time we become completely dependent on technology, which we have already experienced between March and June 2020 when we were confined at home because it was forbidden to go out except to perform basic fundamental tasks or going to work, while others teleworked from home without leaving it most of the time.

But the important questions to ask ourselves are what this data is going to be used for, who is going to use this data, and who is this technology at the service of, to which the globalist oligarchs say they are going to use it for our own benefit, but deep down what they are saying is that they are going to direct our lives because they consider that they have better knowledge of our health than we do. In fact, Klaus Schwab himself paraphrasing says that "the public powers are going to know more than the individuals themselves, and that therefore we will be able to help them in their decision making. "

In fact, it is good that each one is able to make decisions by himself/herself with respect to his own life, while the prohibition of being able to do so or the fact that some other's decisions are imposed on us is simply a deprivation of the fundamental rights of the people.

Thus, the States of the nations and the technological companies are the ones that are going to have access to all this personal data.

In this way, in a release dated February 4, 2021 from the world's most important news agency, the Associated Press, highlights a bill in the state of Nevada that if it goes ahead will allow technology companies to create governments, which has a close relationship with what we have seen in this book in the chapter on inclusive capitalism, which is a project with a global governance system that aims to merge the bad of both worlds, the public and the private in a kind of corporate state that bears more similarities to the totalitarian projects of the 20th century, such as Mussolini's fascism and Hitler's Nazism, than to the so-called social market economy of modern democracies.

This bill in the State of Nevada is led by Democratic Governor Steve Sisolak to launch innovation zones and thus attract investors, which would allow not to local governments, but to technological companies themselves to create their own governments, impose taxes and have the same authority that counties have in the United States.

It is also that all those great economic, social, religious powers that are dedicated to keeping the fruit of our taxes already exist, as it is the case of the Catholic Church in Spain, which takes 1% of Spain's Gross Domestic Product (GDP) through the income tax paid by taxpayers; or as it is the case of the central banks that cover the financial holes of private banks which also pay at the end the taxpayers with their taxes, etc. So it seems that these oligarchs of the technology companies have thought that the path through which the money goes through since the agents of the tax agency take the money out of the pocket of the taxpayers through their taxes to those privileged instances of the world is too long, and they have thought that it would be very good for them if they could shorten the pipeline in such a way that the money would go directly to them, and thus they also save a lot of paperwork, which is easier to do and to achieve in a US State like Nevada where the bureaucracy is much smaller, where there are fewer officials, etc. than in other autonomous communities or nations of the world.

In this way in this type of initiative or at least according to the Nevada project, privileges are granted to the large technology companies because a minimum investment of 1,000 million dollars is required, which not all companies can afford, as it has been established in this bill, that It has not yet gone ahead with but it has already been presented, a project in which one of the companies that has already expressed interest is a company called Blockchains LLC, which should not be confused with the blockchain system, which is the system on which cryptocurrencies are based on. So if they have given to the company the name Blockchains LLC, it seems that they have a clear interest in confusing people about it because otherwise they would give it some other name.

Thus, the company Blockchains LLC, which is dedicated, among other things, to providing digital identity such as the ID2020 project that we have explained in another chapter of the book, using blockchain technology, has a founder named Larry Burns, who has spent years buying lands in this area and who has financed the campaign of the governor who promoted the project through another company called Home Means Nevada Co., whilst he also financed his Republican rival so as not to fail in his financing.

Similarly, Microsoft also patented with an original date of September 21, 2018 a cryptocurrency system that uses body activity data to mine bitcoins and whose process is described as follows: The activity of the human body associated with a task provided to a user can be used in a process of mining a cryptocurrency system. A server can provide a task to a user's device that is communicatively coupled to the server. A sensor communicatively coupled to or comprised of the user's device can detect the user's bodily activity. Body activity data can be generated based on the sensed body activity of the user.

While on the same website of the aforementioned company Blockchains LLC of Larry Burns, which is the first that has signed up for the smart cities with their own government, they already tell us without hiding it that they want to create a new world that will allow the advancement of humanity, which is very reminiscent of a project that is no longer talked about at this moment of the Toronto company Sidewalk Labs, which is a subsidiary of Alphabet, that is to say, of the parent company of Google, and that is a smart city project that was widely announced in its day which was paralyzed after the Canadian Civil Liberties Association (CCLA) took the company to court.

So in order to justify the stoppage of this project, Google or Alphabet have said that due to Covid-19 they have decided not to launch it, when it would be just the opposite that due to the Covid the launching of this project would be accelerated. The fact is that the CCLA has denounced the company Sidewalk Labs for having a project in which infinite data would be collected from the people, which in turn would undermine their rights to privacy and freedom of movement among others, that is what Google wanted to do: to extract data by continuously monitoring residents.

In other words, it would be the same as Google already does through its search engine, but directly providing all the services. So home automation, which is the integration of technology in the intelligent design of a closed room, and in which when someone come backs home, for example, the light is immediately turned on, the curtain is raised, and instructions can be given to the different elements of the house to be turned on or off, will not be necessary with the 5G technology and with the internet of things, since for example it will allow the fridge itself to do the shopping for us because it will decide what to buy based on the parameters that we give it.

In this way many of the procedures that we do both in relation to other elements of the house and in relation to the outside world, most of the latter carried out through the internet will be automated.

So there is no problem and it is not an attack on freedom if at the end people tell the machine what to do and if they wish to depend on that algorithm, whereas if people do not want to depend on the algorithm then they are able to deactivate the machine. But the issue is not really this one but where our data goes.

This already happens today when in Google or Amazon for example we search for something, and then they recommend similar products or services, or when we watch a video on YouTube and then they recommend videos based on what the algorithm interprets that we are interested in, because Google's business is in the user's data, which they call a data surplus.

In fact, it is a surplus of data that comes from the relationship with what we are consulting on the internet, so in the search engine we look for information, we enter some data manually, but also our computer IP, the country in which we are located, our approximate age range depending on the searches carried out, etc. is registered, whilst they consider all of that a surplus of data for which the technological companies do not pay us even though they should do it. That is why these technology companies' client or better said their product is us.

On the other hand, it is possible that some people may think that living in a private city, without state interference and created by the will of individuals is perfect. But it is not at all perfect because it is not a spontaneous order in which resources are allocated based on the decisions of economic agents, but rather a program organized and fed by supranational organizations that actually act as States in the shadow or deep states, which have very specific interests that have nothing to do with ending poverty or having a better relationship with the planet; interests whose objectives may also be achieved more efficiently by creating these prison cities.

So in fact the idea is like in the 1932 dystopian novel "Brave new world" by Adolph Huxley, in which there is a city where everybody is controlled by the elites and everyone is happy anyways because they are being given "happy drugs", even though those elites do with them what they really want and the middle and lower classes do not have any real freedom. This also remembers the case of those ideal cities of the Jesuits in Paraguay, of which there has already been some study in Italy in this regard, and on which a film has also been made about it, such as the 1986 movie "The Mission" with Robert de Niro, which is a great film cinematically speaking, but in which everything that happens is fake, that is it is a totally made up story with the aim of washing up the image of the Jesuits. Thus, in the case of the Jesuits, they even decided in these cities who people would marry to and at what age they would marry.

In fact, an audit of the personal privacy is already taking place through the data that technology collects from people. So we may imagine how terrible that could end up being, since today they are already controlling us mainly through data that we enter voluntarily on our mobile devices or computers; so how worse it will be if they also collect data from us involuntarily while we do any action on our private lives.

So, what is then the role of the citizen in this project?. If we go to the website of the World Economic Forum we are told textually that "the design of cities imposes an order in the socialization of the population, and as technology is linked to the city, it becomes more receptive to its patterns of mobility and interaction. For this reason, it is the responsibility of citizens to participate in political processes to create and safeguard an urban ecosystem that benefits all its inhabitants. "

Therefore by mentioning "an urban ecosystem that benefits all its inhabitants" they are speaking again of the good of the majority versus the individual good, which is a very old idea. That is to say that in the end even if we individuals do not want it, they will implement their project based on the defense of the collective good against the individual good.

Thus, in all the works and in most of the articles of these globalist elites grouped around many brands, they always insist that there is going to be a problem because people will not want to accept their message, and that therefore they will need catalysts.

It is obvious that most people do not want to be monitored 24 hours a day in real time, although someone might want to be monitored all day if they happen to have significant memory losses in order to help them remember to take the medication or to do some other errands for example. In this way there is a lot of talking about "Big Data", that is, massively extracting people's personal data, but what it is really important is the "smart data", which is an evolution of the previous one, because one thing is to massively extract data and another thing is to extract from those data its value to order, categorize and, above all, use it to make decisions.

The ideologues of these elites justify the fact of extracting most of our personal data with the need to detect behavior patterns, needs and desires, which on the contrary we should detect by ourselves or with the help of a psychologist perhaps.

In fact, the ideal would be for them to provide us with the tools to help us achieve these wishes, which the market should take care of with its laws of supply and demand, but as in this case we are not talking about the market or the state but about the interference on people's privacy and will, which is a more serious matter.

All this extracting of the big data is advocated with a scientific justification in which performance and efficiency are always sought above the citizen, who would be in a third or fourth rank.

Noteworthy those who are involved in these projects are the same people over and over again, such as the largest bank in Spain, which is Banco Santander, that participates in a project to convert the capital of the Autonomous Community of Cantabria, which is the city of Santander, in a showcase of the use of technology to optimize public services. In this way it turns out that the city of Santander is the founder of the Spanish Network of Smart Cities, (RECI, according to its Spanish acronym), to which the city of Malaga and some other Spanish cities belong.

In this way with the excuse of using sensors to improve traffic, to improve air quality or at least to detect problems, etc. people are getting used to all this technological control. In addition, most multinationals, at least all Spanish multinationals have also got on that boat, especially now that one of the priority objectives of Spanish companies is to get the rain of millions of euros of public money that the European countries will receive from the European Union through the public spending plan dubbed "Next Generation EU".

In fact, the European Union establishes as conditions for multinationals to receive these millionaire aids to invest in new technologies and make a technological transition. Secondly, that these companies create projects that promote stopping climate change, such as the use of renewable energies.

Thus, technology and climate change are the two key factors to explain this new economic model that they want to impose on us. But when do a little research we discover the true intentions, that is that there are companies that have been working for years to unite the databases of the different organizations, institutions and companies and that are hired by the security services of the countries to use them theoretically in the fight against crime.

In addition, these companies offer support services for the creation and modernization of smart cities, although in fact what they basically do is to collect all the available data and put it at the service of the deep state.

One of these companies that puts together the databases of different organizations, institutions and companies is Palantir Technologies, founded in Denver, Colorado, which became famous because it is the company that was supposed to have helped in locating the Al-Qaeda terrorist, Osama Bin Laden thanks to the use of Big Data, accessing people's mobile phones and satellites. Palantir Technologies was founded in 2003 by one of the founders of Paypal, Peter Thiel, who is another of the usual suspects in the globalist agenda, whose plan when founding this company said that it was to reduce terrorism "while preserving civil liberties ". Although perhaps instead of preserving civil liberties what it is doing is just the opposite if we bear in mind who their clients are.

Among its clients we find the United Nations itself, since what we have just described it is the United Nations urban model designed for the new technocracies, which is at the origin of the 2030 agenda among its sustainable development goals.

In fact, there is a United Nations program called "United for smart sustainable cities", because the United Nations is no more than a transmission belt, that is, they are a transmission belt of the globalist agenda and It does what they order from the top of the globalist pyramid of power.

Specifically, there are 15 UN agencies involved in this project, which is aimed at helping cities achieve the goal of sustainable development, that in turn aims to ensure that cities and human settlements, as can be read on the same website of the UN, are inclusive, safe, resilient and sustainable, which are the 4-5 concepts that are always being repeated in all of the globalist projects.

In fact, on the websites of the globalist entities, their dogmas such as the gender perspective, global warming, the inclusive reception of immigrants may them be legal or not are mixed up, although these concepts have nothing to do with each other and do not even have relationship with the project or the topic that they may be explaining in the article, that is, they add and mix these dogmas and concepts in their articles and speeches like someone would put on a shoe with a shoehorn.

Thus, in an article on the UN website it is said of making a black list of people who are against gender ideology but at the end of the article they also end up talking about global warming, which has no relationship, but both are dogmas of the globalist agenda and each time they cite one of these dogmas they try to add another one.

In fact, on the website of the Great Reset there is a kind of infographic with the title of "Strategic Intelligence" in the shape of a coronavirus or of a big eye depending on how we may see it, which is a structure in which all the concepts of the 2030 globalist agenda are put together, whose propaganda is obviously reaching all corners of the planet. So for example the king of Spain wears the 2030 agenda pin, since most of the politicians, heads of State, private companies, etc. are getting on the boat of the globalist agenda 2030.

Therefore it is a new urban model promoted by the UN and reinforced by the World Economic Forum with the help of satellites, the internet of things and the main technology that facilitates it, which is 5G. So this new urban model with the arrival of the Covid reinforces the propaganda about climate change, that is the inevitable consequence of another old concept which is "smart growth". This concept of smart growth was talked about a lot in the 90s of the 20th century by the theorists of urban planning and transport, many of them heirs of the Fabian thought, who are also in favor of rebuilding society through social engineering.

So, who was going to tell us that they were going to do studies in municipal means of transport with a gender perspective? But this is a reality today and they may even put a machine to certify that these means of transport comply with gender equality and that the same number of men, women and people of other LGTBIQ + genders go on them.

But in the end all this is linked to a concept of technocracy, which in English incorporates an "h" (technocracy), which perhaps better reflects what this concept of technocracy is than other languages, which is the mixture of the government of technicians with the technology governance. Thus, when they began to speak of technocracy, there was still not enough technological development, being the dream of these oligarchies the eye that sees everything, "the Matrix" also in some way in its modern version, although it stems from many ancient myths.

There is a writer named Patrick Wood who has spent years analyzing the emergence of a new political system that merges companies and States, which he especially has written about in his book entitled "Technocracy: The hard road to World Order", explaining that this technocracy is actually these United Nations Sustainable Development Goals, which is a novel vision, but one that explains a lot what is happening under the promise of reforming societies to benefit people.

So the process to benefit people actually hides a reform process to control the people and in this way resources transfer from the hands and property of the people and their representative institutions into the hands of a global common trust operated by the global community elite, says Patrick Wood in the aforementioned book.

Thus when David Rockefeller founded the Trilateral Commission in 1973 to create a new world order, David Wood adds to it that the appropriation of resources had become his master plan and sustainable development somehow became the means to that end.

In this way in order to implement this system, in addition to people not being really aware of the world in which they live, it is also necessary plenty of money that these globalist oligarchies already have in abundance, which they also create it through central banks and private banks; whilst technology is also necessary and is obviously already available. So in the end the last thing that these moguls need in order to implement this system is to have our consent and will, which they are already trying to get.

So we have to understand that the technocrats, those who promote these smart cities using the criteria of sustainability, inclusiveness, efficiency, see human beings as animals, or rather as things, similar to the characters in a video game who are controlled with commands, buttons or joysticks.

Worst of all, many believe that they are actually doing it for the good of humanity and think that the drivers of the Great Reset are the good guys, or that the globalist agenda is directly a conspiracy theory and that it doesn't really exist.

Conclusion

Whether or not we believe in the globalist agenda, it really exists and its promoters continue to develop it through meetings in entities, organizations and institutions with globalist objectives. So concepts with new names appear, be it build back better, sustainable urban development, smart cities, inclusive capitalism, but always the objective is to establish a socialist world government governed by a technocratic elite together with the support of the big technological companies.

Therefore, let us investigate so as not to be confused by these new names, acronyms and projects, because almost always it is about the same actors who are on both sides of the same table planning how to control and subdue the rest of the population that each time will be poorer, less free, while these oligarchies will grow richer and more powerful.

They know that their ideas of global control and surveillance are not to the liking of people, and therefore they hide behind excuses, alleged good intentions, alliances, acronyms and projects to justify and launder their intentions. These are social engineers who want us to see the black white, that is, they want us to see that their control plans are for our own good, but the reality is that they use the collective good againt the individual good in order to be able to restrict our individual rights.

Unfortunately, neither this globalist technocracy seems to be interested in using 5G technology and the internet of things to make us freer or happier, but rather to control and enslave us in "smart cities".

Therefore, let us not let them continue to limit our individual rights with the excuse of the Covid virus or for the defense of the collective good, but let's get up from our seats and protest, demonstrate, and above all, let's go beyond what the official media outlets tell us doing some research on our own on the internet, since we will easily discover that these technocrats are wolves in sheep's clothing who call the black white and the evil good.

Bibliography and sources consulted

- Regarding the Microsoft Alliance for the verification of news together with technological and news corporations in what is called "fact-checking", the information can be read on the Microsoft website itself and in many digital newspapers such as "Libre Mercado" in Spanish at the following link: https://www.libremercado.com/2021-03-02/bill-gates-ministerio-verdad-microsoft-internet-verificador-fake-news-6714523/

- Programs of the Great Reset with César Vidal and Lorenzo Ramírez on the César Vidal TV platform about inclusive capitalism, the world of Bill Gates and the smart cities.

- Regarding the multinationals, foundations and NGOs that are mentioned in this book, all their information is publicly accessible through their own web pages on the internet.

- Regarding the mentions of articles and videos of the International Economic Forum, everything can be found on its website: https://www.weforum.org

For example, regarding Strategic Intelligence, the information can be found on this page: https://intelligence.weforum.org/, and regarding Sustainable Cities and Communities, the information can be found on this page:
https://intelligence.weforum.org/topics/a1G0X0000057N1IUAU?tab=publications

- Regarding the experiments that are being carried out with human beings with the Covid-19 vaccines, the news has been extracted from the Telegram channel "El Arconte". Thus, in relation to the Pfizer vaccine the information can be found on this page: https://clinicaltrials.gov/ct2/show/NCT04368728

In relation to the Moderna vaccine the information can be found at this link:
https://clinicaltrials.gov/ct2/show/NCT04470427

The news about the human experiments with the Covid-19 vaccines in Spanish can be found in this link from the newspaper "El diestro":https://www.eldiestro.es/2021/04/para-los-que-todavia-no-se-crean-que-vacunajando-estan-participando-en-un-experimento-vean-cuando-finaliza-la- modern-and-pfizer-experimentation-according-to-an-official-website-of-the-us-government /

- Regarding the Microsoft patent of a system in which the data of the human body connected to sensors is used to mine cryptocurrencies, the information can be found in this link:

https://patentscope.wipo.int/search/en/detail.jsf;jsessionid=4C1AEC7CA06D76234508FE22C8968E19.wapp2nC?docId=WO2020060606&tab=PCTBIBLIO